TO:

_____

FROM:

_____

LAUGHING
THROUGH THE
UGLY CRY

AND FINDING
UNSTOPPABLE

JOY

DAWN BARTON

THOMAS NELSON

Since 1798

Published in Nashville, Tennessee, by Thomas Nelson. Thomas Nelson is a registered trademark of HarperCollins Christian Publishing, Inc.

Interior Photography: Ashley Victoria Photography www.ashleyvictoria.com

Scripture quotations are taken from the Holy Bible, New International Version®, NIV®. Copyright © 1973, 1978, 1984, 2011 by Biblica, Inc.® Used by permission of Zondervan. All rights reserved worldwide. www.Zondervan.com. The "NIV" and "New International Version" are trademarks registered in the United States Patent and Trademark Office by Biblica, Inc.®

Scripture quotations marked MSG are taken from *The Message*. Copyright © by Eugene H. Peterson 1993, 1994, 1995, 1996, 2000, 2001, 2002. Used by permission of NavPress. All rights reserved. Represented by Tyndale House Publishers, Inc.

Any internet addresses, phone numbers, or company or product information printed in this book are offered as a resource and are not intended in any way to be or to imply an endorsement by Thomas Nelson, nor does Thomas Nelson vouch for the existence, content, or services of these sites, phone numbers, companies, or products beyond the life of this book.

ISBN 978-1-4002-1776-2 (HC)
ISBN 978-1-4002-1774-8 (audiobook)
ISBN 978-1-4002-1777-9 (eBook)

Printed in China
20 21 22 23 24 SKY 5 4 3 2 1

FOR MY DAUGHTERS,
MAKENZIE AND ELLASON
FOREVER MY JOY

CONTENTS

A NON-READER'S TAKE ON JOY

I WASN'T MUCH OF a book person when I set out to write a book. I'm still not. I can count the books I've read cover to cover on one hand, and most were stories I read to children under the age of five. Reading has never been my strength, my pastime, or my gift. Give me the quick overview—the first two chapters—and I'm good to go.

Yes, I do *know* people who read. Heck, I'm related to some who are voracious readers. My mother and husband read book after book and intentionally purchase books with more than 250 pages. Baffling, isn't it?

I'd like to be one of those voracious readers, mostly because I want to say the word *voracious* when discussing my reading prowess.

I'm just not that girl. And I'm here to tell you that there are

more of us than you might think. I have two friends who are successful authors, and neither is a reader. So trust me: it's a thing.

To be clear, I do buy books—*lots* of books. I never finish them,
but I buy them. If I borrow a book, the pressure to read is huge.
But if I purchase a book, I don't feel as morally obligated to read it.
I mean, it's mine, right? I can do whatever I want with it.

I think what it comes down to is that I have the attention span
of a gnat. (I wonder if gnats actually have a huge attention span. In
the world of tiny, annoying bugs, what if gnats are actually the *best*
at focusing? Are they the great thinkers, the philosophers of their
kind? PS: These are the deep, important questions you can expect
to find in this book. Congratulations on your wise investment.) You
get my point. It's a bit ironic that the girl who doesn't read a ton
would write a book.

Now that I've revealed this big secret and shown a truckload
of vulnerability the way Brené Brown told me to, you know the
truth from my perspective: you can buy *a lot* of books and not be
a huge reader.

Even though this non-reader has finally written a book, it's okay
if you don't finish it, but you should, because the end is particularly
inspiring. Yes, I did that on purpose to push you. All you three-
chapter champs, get ready. We're going all the way, baby!

Look, I may not have a PhD in English literature, but I do

consider myself a highly qualified Joyologist. That's a scientific discipline (founded by myself) where we look for joy in the most unfriendly, unlikely, inhospitable places. You wouldn't believe where joy can grow and survive. I've seen it for myself, in my own story. Strike that—in many, *many* of my stories. And though I haven't read profusely and I certainly haven't written profusely, I *do* have stories. So yes—I've written them down in a book. I don't know whether to call some of these stories comedies or tragedies, but all of them are about finding belly laughs even through the ugliest of ugly cries. About spotting joy, even if you have to haul out a microscope.

This is a book of hope. Every time I have chosen to start climbing out a dark hole (and yes, I believe it is a choice), I have found little, unexpected pieces of hope, like breadcrumbs leading me slowly, slowly, slowly toward the light. I hope that as you read them, you'll find a little light for yourself.

> **I'VE REALIZED THAT IN THE DARKEST HOLES OF LIFE, THERE IS JOY.**

CATHOLIC LITE

Faith That Can't Be Bullied by Life

Faith. It does not make things easy.
It makes them possible.

I WAS RAISED CATHOLIC-LITE. We were Catholic, but we didn't go to church much. In my parents' defense, we grew up all over the world, moving from country to country (my dad was in the oil business), so there wasn't a whole lot of predictability in our Sundays. In some places, it was easy to attend church. In others, like Iran, not so much.

I didn't ponder my faith often, but I knew I loved God. I had no idea why; I just did. We didn't have Bible readings or Scripture discussions in our home. We believed in God, we knew that Jesus was His Son, and we also thought a third party called the Holy Spirit was very nice. I knew this because when I made the sign of the cross, we listed three things: "In the name of the Father, and of the Son, and of the Holy Spirit. Amen."

Three. Got it. Love 'em. Okay.

Like many things in my life, my relationship with God has evolved throughout a fairly turbulent life journey. It began in my youth with that innocent, unquestioning faith. In my early twenties, it transitioned to a full-on, plates-smashed-against-walls kind of anger and a "breakup" with God (you'll understand why in a moment). Then it moved into a cautious, slow "dating period" in my late twenties until I was *all in* with God in my thirties.

I gave my life to God at thirty-nine—totally, utterly, and completely. I mean, not like a monk who gives up every bit of his worldly goods or something, but my heart and soul became His. It was *very* clear that God had not called me to give up my laptop or cell phone.

So what precipitated the breakup?

The plate-breaking years began in 1989. I was the ripe old age of nineteen when I fell in love, married a wonderful man, and started having babies. In my world, this was the be-all and end-all for a good Southern girl. I was set for my happily ever after. Of course,

we were young and struggled as most young couples do—with our finances, our communication, our approaches to parenting, all of it. We were babies trying to be grown-ups and raising two precious little ones, Makenzie and Madison.

In June 1991, our lives were completely shattered. We lost our precious daughter Madison to a rare bacterial pneumonia. She was nine months old. One week she was pressing her sweet face into the curve of my neck and beginning to pull up into a standing position, and eight days later she was in my arms taking her last breath in a tiny pediatric ICU room at Saint Francis Hospital. It happened so cruelly fast.

THROUGH OUR YOUTHFUL MESS, WE FOUND HAPPINESS.

I have the most vivid memory of sitting in Madison's bedroom one August night, eight weeks after she was gone. Every piece of clothing still hanging in her closet, the plush stuffed animals resting in the corners of her room, but her crib stood empty. I was pushing myself back and forth in her rocking chair, crying a cry so intense it wracked every muscle in my body and sucked up every ounce of air in my lungs. It felt like all the tears I could make in an entire lifetime were flowing in that moment. The pain was so excruciating that I could barely gasp for breath.

It's been twenty-five years. I can still smell the scent of her room. I can see the vibrant colors of the mural on her wall. I can feel the softness of her sheets and blankets—all of it etched in my mind for an eternity. I still remember how angry I felt that my husband was in the other room, unable to comfort me or even himself. But most of all I was furious that I had loved a God who took babies away from their mommies. I would never breathe normally after this, and I would never again love this God.

My husband and I were forever, dramatically, and drastically changed. Within two months of losing her, we separated. Neither of us knew how to deal with the pain and anger of Madison's loss.

Then, just four months later, my world was ravaged in an entirely different way. On December 2, I woke up in the middle of the night to an elbow on my chest and a hand slapping down, covering my mouth. A man had broken into my home. His face was inches from my own, his eyes staring into mine. I could feel his breath as he whispered, "If you don't do what I tell you to do, I will hurt you."

My daughter Makenzie, three years old, was sleeping next to me. *Please, dear God,* I prayed, *don't let her wake up.* The man allowed me to take her, still sleeping, to her room.

He pulled me back to my room and onto my bed. "Take off your clothes," he said with a cold, commanding voice.

With tears flowing down my face and my fingers gripped in a

praying position, I whispered the Lord's Prayer over and over. Then, as clear as I have ever heard anything, I heard God: "You are going to be fine. You are going to make it through this. *I am here.*"

God was there, and I did get through that unimaginable experience. My rapist was caught that night and, to this day, is serving a life sentence in prison. But my life was changed in a way I never imagined possible, and I became a woman I didn't know. I was fearful of everything and felt scared just navigating daily activities. I spent countless hours in therapy. I was a disastrous mess of a human being.

In the years to come, I would fall in love, get married, and have another daughter. But I would find myself in an ugly cry again and again. I would later be diagnosed with Stage 3, triple-negative breast cancer while my new husband, Craig, was in Bahrain with the Navy. We would battle addiction and have struggles in our own home. My mother would have a ruptured brain aneurysm that would nearly take her life, and I would lose my baby sister unexpectedly to breast cancer.

So, in all these trials, how was I supposed to find joy?

As you can see, joy wasn't exactly flowing into my life. But this is exactly why I know the life-saving power of *seeking* joy. Through losing my sweet Madison, a divorce from a good and kind man, and a rape that would go to a full jury trial, joy came in the form of my three-year-old bundle of love, Makenzie. (I was twenty-three, she was three, and we would raise each other for a while. But, boy, did we have joy.) Through all that followed with my new husband, my mother, and my sister, I found joy in humor and people and countless moments of unpredictable truths.

I don't bring up the topic of joy lightly, and I know it's not always easy to seek joy or allow laughter. My heart has been broken so many times, in so many tiny pieces, that I have at times felt certain it would never heal. I've been sure the sun would never shine again and that I'd never get out of bed. Maybe you've felt the same.

There is no play-by-play guide to being joyful when you're in pain. Hurting is hurting. I know that feeling of not being able to stop crying, of having wept so much that it seems like your body shouldn't be able to produce one more tear. I know how it feels to be furious at the world, helplessly thinking over and over, *This can't be happening. This isn't real.* I know how it feels when you think that you'll never recover, that you'll never emerge from the darkness, and that your life is most certainly over.

> **THERE IS NO PLAY-BY-PLAY GUIDE TO BEING JOYFUL WHEN YOU'RE IN PAIN.**

I've been there. I understand. If that's you, I hear you.

But I want you to know joy can be found inside the tsunami of pain. My prayer is that my stories help you see that joy isn't always where we expect it or how we expect it, but it *is* there in tiny, unexpected ways.

Our stories, the good and the bad, make us who we are. They give us character. They allow us to identify and empathize with others—to connect, on big and small levels. I don't believe any of us were born to sit back in silence and just exist. We weren't created to live lives of sadness, anger, or depression. We weren't made for blaming, withholding forgiveness, or being negative. We were made to find the gift of joy.

But how do we spot it? When I had cancer, I found out that joy is laughing so hard about your ugly new chemo hat with your friends that one of you pees in her pants. Joy is realizing you don't have to cook for two months because someone set up a meal train for you. Joy is the moment, years after you're completely healthy and people expect you to start cooking again, when you proclaim that you'll never roast a ham again because, actually, you hate to cook. Moments of joy are often sprinkled into the most unlikely places.

In my forty-nine years of life, I've learned that joy and pain often go hand in hand. I believe I have experienced more joy than many people ever will because I have experienced more pain than

most will. But that's why you can believe me when I tell you: even if everything is falling apart, you *can* find laughter again.

Once I understood this, I knew I had something to share, something for God to use. God loves working through flawed, messed-up humans. (Don't believe me? Read the Bible!) And our God is more than just the nice, fatherly figure I learned about in my "Catholic-lite" days. He gets involved. He heals. He loves to bring us out of the brokenness, to give us a new story, a new beginning. He's the King of the comeback story. (I mean, there will never be a better comeback story than Jesus. Literally and figuratively.)

> **WHEN WE CHOOSE TO SEEK THE JOY, IT'S ALWAYS THERE TO BE FOUND.**

Life is a wild, magnificent journey mixed with lessons, loss, pain, and beautiful, astonishing *joy*. In your own pain and seasons of tears, how will joy and laughter sneak in through the cracks? How will they surprise you, or give you the relief you didn't think you'd ever have again? Let that hope spark up in you. You'll have joy again. Here are a few stories of how it happened for me.

I'M NOT YOUR GIRL

Jumping Without a Net

When I am afraid, I put my trust in you.

PSALM 56:3

"YOU ARE NOT QUALIFIED to write about God." That message plays over and over in my head like a broken record.

Even as I write these words, I do not feel ready. I'm no theologian. I have no formal biblical education, and I have not read the Bible cover to cover. (I've come close, but all of those "the son of, the son of, the son of" parts are really hard to get through!) I've never spontaneously quoted Scripture, although I do know many verses. They just don't seem to pop out quickly enough when I need them. I sound more like, "You know, there's this part in the Bible where . . ."

My past (and sometimes my current) behavior also disqualifies me. My twenties were unrestrained, with enough alcohol consumption to make a college fraternity on spring break look tame. I have gossiped, I have judged others, I have yelled at my child when we were going to church in a way that should've made lightning strike me the moment I walked through the doors. At times I have been a bad wife, daughter, and friend. I have broken trust, and I have let people down more times than I care to say. I am not the vision of goodness or righteousness. I am highly flawed, messed up, insecure, and seriously out of shape.

In short, I am not qualified to write about God . . . or am I?

Now, I don't know if you know much about the Bible, but pretty much every person God used was not qualified for what He called them to do. Not just a little unqualified, but so completely on the opposite side that you're absolutely sure there is no way they could become a champion for God. So when I sit back and think about it, I'm in pretty good company.

Noah was a drunk. Abraham was too old. Jacob was a liar. Joseph was abused. Moses had a stuttering problem (and argued with God *a lot*. Unfortunately, I do this too.). Gideon was afraid. Samson was a womanizer. Rahab was a prostitute. David was an adulterer and a murderer. Jonah ran from God. Peter denied Christ. And these are just a handful! God calls the unqualified and qualifies them.

While others were receiving beautiful Christian educations and in-depth theological training, I was getting what I like to call "on-the-job training" from God. You know by now that my life seems to have had a continued pattern of trials and tragedies. For decades, it has felt as if one trial would end and another would begin.

GOD CALLS THE UNQUALIFIED AND QUALIFIES THEM.

But with each trial, I moved further along a winding road that eventually led to a deep faith in God. My faith wasn't consistent, nor did it reliably inch upward like the mark on a child's growth chart. Instead, it zigzagged. I wavered, I questioned, and I doubted until, eventually, I knew I loved God with all that I was and would ever be.

Looking back on that wild road of my faith, I believe it was *because I did* waver, question, and doubt that I am qualified to share this with you today. God loved me, even when I turned from Him. This took me so long to learn, but in the craziest of ways, it's part of what qualifies me to write this book and share what I am sharing with you.

> LOOKING BACK ON THAT WILD ROAD OF MY FAITH, I BELIEVE IT WAS *BECAUSE I DID* WAVER THAT I AM QUALIFIED TO SHARE THIS TODAY.

As I matured in my life and faith, I learned to talk to God, to pray to Him, and to reach out to Him more and more. I needed Him and I knew it. I needed Him to hold my hand, and sometimes I needed Him to wrap His arms all the way around me and hold me tight until I was ready to face the world again. I needed Him to take my sorrow and give me peace and joy—and He did.

I came to know God in the most intimate and beautiful way:

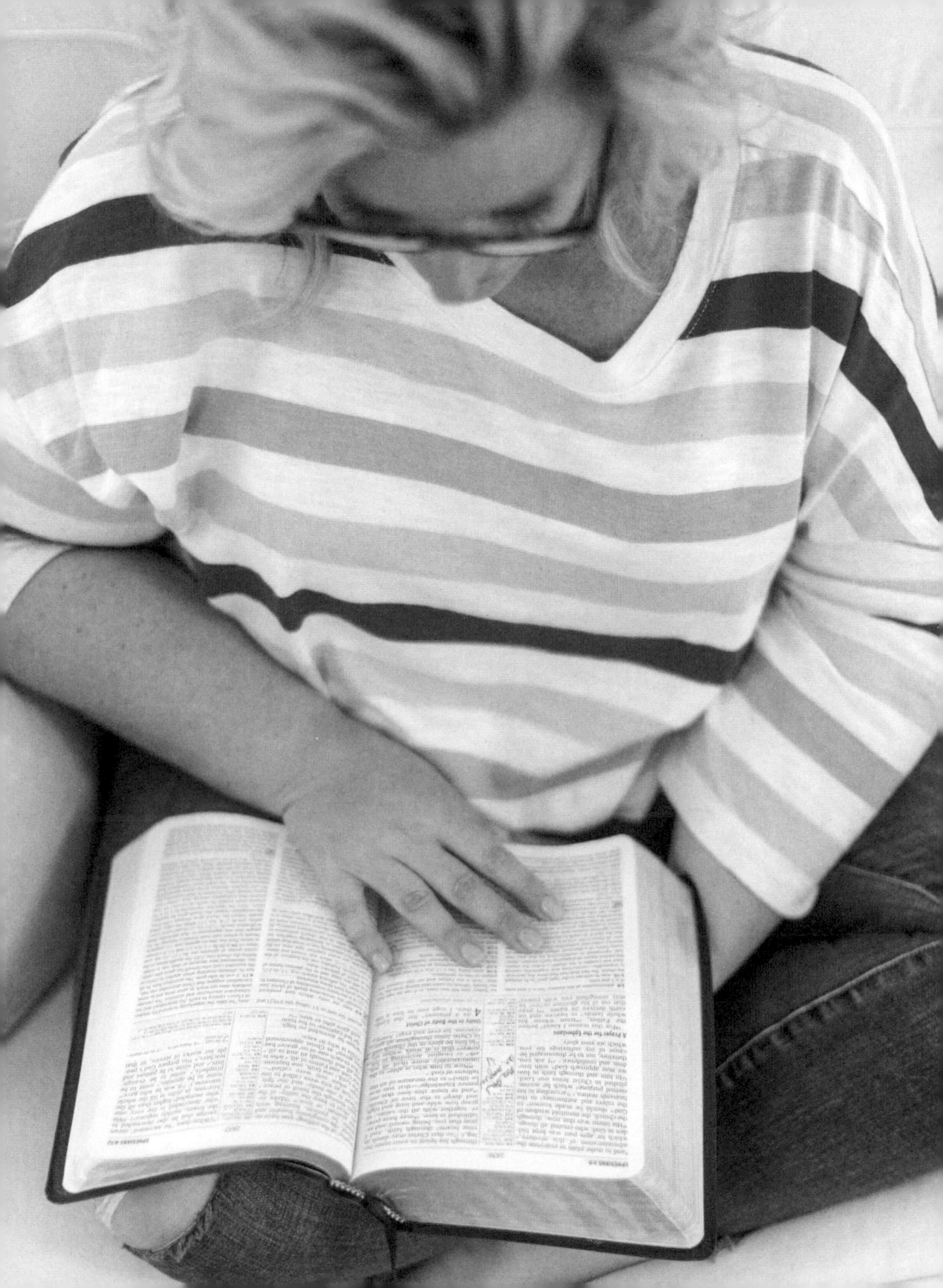

through the valleys of my life, not on the mountaintops, and not in a classroom or at Sunday school.

Two years ago, when I began to tell people about a book I was working on, they repeatedly asked, "Who are you writing the book for?"

The answer was always a fast and simple one: "Me, fifteen years ago." Fifteen years ago, I wouldn't have been open to hearing Scripture or having deep, spiritual conversations. I was just beginning to stick my toe into the water of faith, and I would have been scared off with talk of too much "religion."

I was so hardened from the previous ten years, but slowly, my heart opened to the thought of a relationship with the God I had casually known when I was younger. If you'd have asked me back then how I felt about God, I would've told you I loved the idea of Him, but I had no idea I could actually have a relationship with Him.

> I WANT YOU TO KNOW YOU CAN BE MAD AT GOD, BECAUSE HE CAN TAKE IT.

Fifteen years ago, the thought that God loved Dawn Barton, the woman who cursed Him, turned from Him, and doubted Him, was more than my mind could fathom. Sure, I figured He could love me a little, maybe, but not wildly and passionately. That sort of love was reserved for the good Scripture-quoting Christians of the world.

I want to reach *that* girl.

I want to reach anyone with an ounce of doubt about how much God loves you. Even when your life is hard, even in the times when it feels like He isn't there, I want you to know He is. I want you to know you can be mad at Him, because He can take it. You can yell and you can cry out. He can take it. You can question, *Why me? Why did I get dealt a horrible hand? Why has my life been so much worse?* It's okay. He can take it.

Nothing you say, nothing you do will stop His love from being poured out on you. My greatest desire for this book is that you will open your mind and heart to God, because in God there is joy. The truth is, they are one: joy is God, and God is joy. Because joy with and through God is different—it's divine joy.

When God calls you, He *will* equip you. All He is asking is that you trust Him and take one step forward. Take His hand and take one step.

JOY IS GOD, AND GOD IS JOY.

If you're considering taking a leap of faith to answer a God calling, but you're feeling unqualified and nervous about the unknown, let me leave you with an analogy that might give you hope.

For those of you who are mothers, remember that moment you learned you were carrying a child inside you? For some, it was an answer to many prayers, and you were utterly filled with joy. For others, myself included, it was more like, "Are you sure? My parents are going to be so mad. The wedding isn't for another six months, and they're going to kill me." Yes, you heard right. My big cathedral wedding had to be moved up several months, and it wasn't because I was the next Blessed Mother Mary.

Whether you prayed for a pregnancy or not, you can panic when it comes to birthing babies and entering parenthood. *I am not equipped. I am not ready. There is no way I should be trusted to raise a human, much less a tiny one.*

But, before you know it, a precious child is put in your arms and all is right with the world. God has never been more *God* than in this moment, and He has never created a more perfect child than this one. You are not sure if you are equipped to be a good mother, but you are certain you will never love anything more than this beautiful, tiny body in your arms.

Truth be told, none of us is equipped for parenthood with a first child. Not for their bodily functions, their sleepless nights, their bloodcurdling screams—not even for the depths our love grows for them each day (until the teenage years), or the intensity of how much we hurt when they hurt. And nothing on God's green earth equips us for mommy guilt, the single most powerful weapon in the world.

And yet, day by day, we make it. We stretch in our thinking, in our gifts, and in our capacity for love. With each passing day, we are equipped for the task of parenthood a little more. We go from being totally inexperienced to totally qualified, simply by doing it. In this same way, God equips us for that which He calls us to do. Little by little, step by step, He gives us the tools we need when we need them.

Now, that sounds lovely and sweet, but I'm here to tell you it's not that pretty, sister. I am going to request that God please give me a business plan and some detailed spreadsheets with my next calling, should He ever see fit to call me into something again. A lot of

> GOD EQUIPS US FOR THAT WHICH HE CALLS US TO DO. LITTLE BY LITTLE, STEP BY STEP, HE GIVES US THE TOOLS WE NEED WHEN WE NEED THEM.

tears, doubt, and heartache could have been avoided with some better communication and a little color-coded spreadsheet. Just sayin'.

However, I will admit—though sheepishly—the growth and all the good, juicy stuff is in the journey. It's in those valleys, in the failures and skinned knees from repeated falls. It's in the hurt and in the pain that He sharpens us, teaches us, and loves us.

I still don't *feel qualified* to write this book or talk about God, and I don't know that I ever will. But I do know this: living a life only doing things we are qualified to do would be incredibly boring, and let's be real, you'd probably be pretty boring too. No substance, no good stories, no lessons to learn from and to teach from.

My advice: Take a leap of faith whenever you can and listen to the little voice nudging you (not the one that tells you to eat chocolate cakes, the other one—God). Let God lead you, and choose to trust Him in that leading. God is in the process of qualifying you right this minute—and He has definitely called you to something extraordinary. So whether you feel qualified or not, just jump. You won't be sorry.

CANCER SCHMANCER

Choosing How the Story Goes

Be joyful in hope, patient in affliction, faithful in prayer.

ROMANS 12:12

IT WAS A GIFT. I don't know how else to say it. Cancer was a strange, unexpected gift.

There is life before cancer and life after cancer, but life after cancer is just better. Granted, my body may not be better (today I caught myself thinking, *When can I schedule surgery to get that right nipple put on?*), but my life certainly is.

When I used to think about the big lessons life would offer

21

me, I envisioned curling up at my grandparents' feet and taking in tales of wisdom. Or maybe I'd sit in a large leather chair by a huge window and have epiphany-filled moments while I perused Bible verses and gazed at the wild waves of the sea. (I don't actually have a sea outside my window, but that visual makes for a vivid, deep-thought moment.) I never once imagined my biggest life lessons would come while being bald and sick as my breast was slowly consumed by cancer. And yet, that circumstance is exactly how a lot of wisdom came my way.

I got hard, intense lessons about life while I was in a lot of pain. I learned more about who I was as a woman and how all of us can use our beautiful gifts in this life. Best of all: Through cancer, my faith exploded.

CANCER ISN'T IMMUNE TO A GOOD COMEDIC TAKEDOWN.

The most unexpected part of the journey was learning cancer isn't immune to a good comedic takedown. I won't dilute this by saying something trite like, "Laughter is the best medicine." But if I were the kind of person who relied on clichés to capture a simple truth, that's the one I would use. I learned to laugh at myself, even when circumstances were dire, and to appreciate everything right in front of me.

Cancer is horrible. Don't think for a moment I don't know that. It can ravage your body, it can knock you to the ground in seconds, it can take your life. But here's what I want you to know: in spite of cancer's vile destruction, you can also find beauty and laughter when you look for them.

Just to be clear, I never want to have cancer again, gifts or no gifts. I'm happy now. I like my hair again. I like my one old boob and one new boob. And, just between us, I don't even mind my uni-nipple.

Let me tell you how all this started. It was March of 2011 when my husband came home on leave from the Navy. I could hardly contain myself. *He was home!* My beloved, my friend, my husband was back on US soil. It was only for two weeks, but I was going to soak up every single ounce of Craig Barton.

I had missed everything about him—the way he felt, the way he sounded, the scent of his deodorant. I missed it all. Wait . . . in regard to scents, I would like to go on record and say I did *not* miss the odor of his Sanuk shoes. No human could miss the gag-inducing scent of decaying feet that filled the room the moment he slid out of them. But there was no need to replace those beauties because—according to Craig—they were "perfectly fine and just needed to be thrown in the washing machine."

Other than those shoes and their unfortunate effect on my husband's feet, I missed it all. He was finally here, finally home, and my heart was full.

I had decided our two weeks together would be the best fourteen days of his entire life. I planned 336 hours of adventure, romance, and family fun with the precision of a perky 1980s travel agent and a Pinterest wedding planner, all rolled into one. A couple of nights at a plush beach hotel, Disney World with our daughter for a few days, visits with our closest family, and nights out with our coolest friends. Six months of missed life *smooshed* into two weeks.

Of course, this was all my idea, definitely not my husband's. Craig would have preferred to spend his vacation in our living room, sitting in his favorite oversized chair and flipping through our 265 channels while he snacked on chips and salsa—with those stinky Sanuks kicked off somewhere by the front door. But in the midst of my glorious planning, I may have forgotten to ask what *he* wanted to do. Oops.

We started the festivities by checking into the hotel, where our gorgeous room overlooked the sugary white sands and immaculate teal water of our hometown beach. When it was time to get ready for dinner with our friends, I was bringing my A game. This meant taking a shower *and* doing my hair. No sexy ponytail for this Navy man, no ma'am. I was pulling out the big guns: the blow-dryer and the curling iron.

My hair is thick and takes an eternity to dry, so deciding to wrestle my hair into submission was out of the norm. My hands were in the air, pulling, brushing, and teasing my hair for maximum height. (As we say in the South, the bigger the hair, the closer to God.) Finally, I pulled the hairbrush through to the ends for the finishing stroke. As my hand came down, my wrist brushed the top of my right breast. I felt a large lump. It was large enough that I could grab it with two fingers. How had I missed this? What on earth was it?

Fifteen minutes later, our friends arrived downstairs for dinner. As luck would have it, one of them was a radiologist—exactly the person I needed. She told me to come to her office on Monday morning and she would scan me.

Five days into our dreamy, romantic two weeks, I was walking into the radiology department of Sacred Heart Hospital, and within an hour, my friend was performing an ultrasound on my right breast. She stared at the film of my scan over and over, then asked

> AS WE SAY IN THE SOUTH, THE BIGGER THE HAIR, THE CLOSER TO GOD.

if I would stay for a mammogram. I entered the room for the mammogram, got pulled and squashed for a few minutes, and then it was done. (If you have not had a mammogram, they are super fun and you should get one. Think closing a garage door on your boob while somebody watches. Ten out of ten, would do it again!)

After the mammogram, my friend read the scans and consulted with another doctor. Both agreed the large lump was made up of cysts, but that they were harmless and would probably go away. Wonderful news! I was thrilled to get home to Craig so I could continue to torture him with more fun.

Weeks later, Craig was back in Bahrain for his military assignment, and I headed to another doctor's office—this time to my ob-gyn for a scheduled annual checkup. My doctor, another amazing and accomplished woman, didn't like the feel of the lump on my breast, and she insisted on another mammogram and ultrasound. Once more, both scans showed cysts. But this time my doctor was very uneasy about the *feel* of the mass. She called the next day, a Friday morning, and shared her concerns. She wanted me to have a biopsy done first thing the following week.

Tuesday morning I arrived at the same office where I'd had my earlier mammograms and ultrasounds. A sweet friend, Kelli, insisted on driving me to the procedure, and although I felt abnormally calm given the circumstances, it was nice to have the company.

THIS TIME MY DOCTOR WAS VERY UNEASY ABOUT THE *FEEL* OF THE MASS.

Somehow I've made friends with a ton of radiologists, and three of them practiced at this clinic. This time, however, I didn't know the doctor performing the biopsy, but I was assured that he (yes, this one was a man) was great.

After ten minutes of sitting in the waiting room with my friend, a door opened and a nurse called me back. She left me in a room to change into the ever-fashionable hospital gown. I changed, sat, and waited, this time without Kelli to laugh and cut up with me. A few minutes later, a new nurse opened the door wearing purple scrubs. She began to tell me about the procedure I was about to have. It sounded interesting, but it wasn't the one I was scheduled for. I explained I was there for a biopsy. The nurse argued back, with the kind of irritated edge that comes from jumping on a scale in the morning and seeing an unexpected five-pound weight gain. It's a heaviness that stays with a woman all day. I know it well.

As we argued, the doctor walked in and clarified I was indeed having a biopsy, thus ending our heated debate. He guided us into the procedure room, where my nurse carried on with her lovely demeanor. She refused to make eye contact with me and gave me short, curt commands. She was obviously not happy about being wrong. I, however, was doing an extravagant mental dance inside my head—arms flailing, pointing in her face, singing, *Told you so, told you so!* It made me happier than it should have.

Inside the room I saw a raised hospital bed in the corner, a tray with surgical tools, and what looked like a wall-mounted television. My nurse—let's call her "Joy" for fun—instructed me to get on the bed and lie down on my side. It was an awkward position: on my side, a little twisted at the hip, arm draped above my head so that my breast was perfectly balanced and pointing directly at the ceiling—kind of like balancing a Jell-O mold. Think Kate Winslet in *Titanic* getting sketched by Leo. It's the sexy position that all women know. No one actually lies down like this for comfort, but we think it makes us look really good.

Joy draped me with a sterile cloth that had an opening around my breast; then they numbed the breast area and turned on the television screens. My doctor explained that he was just going to stick the needle in and attempt to burst the cysts. As the ultrasound transducer glided across my breast, an image appeared on the screen. I could see the needle enter the breast toward what looked like three round circles. As the needle moved closer to the circular shapes, he explained he was going to glide into the cysts and aspirate them.

But when he touched the cyst, it did not burst at all. He made several attempts, poking at the other cysts, and nothing. His facial expression changed and, worst of all, so did Joy's. Her demeanor shifted dramatically as she tilted her head and looked into my eyes with a soft, compassionate smile. "You're doing great," she said gently. This was not a good sign.

The doctor continued and performed a biopsy, which consisted of taking pieces of the tissue out of the circular shapes. As he finished, I felt blood, lots of blood, running down my breast and onto my neck. A thought fell into my head with a thud: *Cancer bleeds a lot.* It was a phrase I had heard at some point. *Cancer bleeds a lot. I am bleeding a lot. This is not good.* No one said anything, but the doctor and Joy continued to be overly kind and coddling, a combination that made me increasingly wary.

Joy let me know we would have the results the next day. I returned to the dressing room, put on my clothes, met Kelli out front, and started to walk out. Before we'd even made it to the car, I got a text from one of my radiology friends:

"Are you okay? I heard it didn't go well."

I looked at the text and thought, *I think I just found out I have cancer over a text message.*

I don't know why, perhaps it was the shock of it all, but I chuckled.

We got in the car and I turned to Kelli. "Well," I said, "I'm pretty sure I have breast cancer."

The next day the results were in and my fears were confirmed: invasive ductal carcinoma.

Breast cancer.

Over the next four days, I would learn that my cancer was already in Stage 3 out of 4 and that I had a less-common type that was known to be more aggressive than most others—triple negative. It's a cancer not fed by hormones, and that's bad. The cancer had already spread to my lymph nodes, and it was beginning to make its way into other areas of my body when we caught it.

It was one heck of a diagnosis. It was a diagnosis I did not feel ready for—not that anyone ever does—and I knew fighting this monster was going to get ugly.

But, as with most things in my life, it was also going to get a little ridiculous. So let's talk about those first couple of weeks, the chaotic pace and cringey moments that kicked off my cancer journey.

As soon as I got diagnosed, things went into hyperdrive, from attending doctors' appointments to having blood work and getting scans to scheduling surgeries. My first two scans were a breast MRI and a PET scan.

Before the PET scan, I was injected with a liquid they called *contrast*. The contrast allows abnormalities to show on the films more clearly. After the contrast goes in, but before the scan, it is vitally important that you stay very, very still.

For one hour, I had to sit without speaking or moving. I was alone in a room with no phone, no TV. I had to be still so the contrast would be exactly where it needed to be when it came time for the scan. "Still and calm," they said. "Stay still and calm." And they left me alone, just me and my thoughts.

If I'm ever captured by the enemy, this is what they should use as torture to get me to talk.

For days leading up to the appointment, I had been pounded by relentless appointment-making and terrifying information that was preparing me for the battle against cancer, but the sheer speed in which it was unfolding had kept me so occupied that there hadn't been time to overanalyze my life. Until then.

I sat there, being still and feeling everything—sadness over what lay ahead, anger and fury at this poison spreading in my body. My mind buzzed with a million thoughts, from the complex to the ridiculous. I shouldn't have eaten so much fast food. I should have exercised. I should have drunk more water—unless, wait, is my water bad? Did I get cancer from my water? Or my cell phone or my bra? Why on earth is this happening to me?

I felt angry that my body hadn't warned me, that I didn't have any signs (well, aside from the massive tumor sticking out of my

chest). I'd always believed if I were to get some potentially fatal disease, I would know. I would be so in tune with my body that I would feel it. But I didn't have some inexplicable fatigue or sickness or a cold . . . nothing. I was fine. In fact, I felt better than fine. I was energetic and busy.

Receiving a breast cancer diagnosis almost seems cliché now. The numbers are staggering: one in every eight women will develop breast cancer, and only 10 percent of those women have a family history of breast cancer. But like falling in love or tasting a Mississippi Mud Pie for the first time, even the most universal event is profoundly stunning, unique, and life-altering when it happens to you.

Looking back, I see part of me could laugh during my initial medical appointments and prognosis because I didn't fully understand the magnitude of what was going on inside me. Later, I wasn't so amused as I came to understand the cancer had moved outside of the breast, into the lymph nodes, and was growing throughout my body.

But as I looked at those films of my body, it wasn't just naivete that allowed me to laugh; it was a *choice* to be willing to find the joy. I know this because, as time passed and I began to understand cancer's awfulness, I was still able to laugh. I had to.

Let's be clear: learning you have Stage 3 cancer does 100

percent suck. I wish I could sugarcoat it, but I can't. I wish no one ever had to hear the words "you have cancer" or any other announcement that cuts through you like a knife. But if and when you do, I pray you'll realize the choice you have.

You get to decide what your story will look like and how to design your life.

I decided cancer did *not* get to be the maestro of some sad symphony playing the soundtrack of my life. Instead, I pictured cancer as a dirty, smelly river running across the road of my glorious life, and I had to wade through it to get to something even better on the other side. And believe it or not, dredging through those murky, nasty waters turned out to be a blessing.

Even in the face of all the things you can't control—the announcements, the diagnoses, the calls you hoped you'd never get—there's something you do get to control. Choose to let it give you wisdom. Choose to look for joy in the midst of it and grab onto it. Be willing to find joy in the small spaces between the fear and confusion, and make *that* the moral of your story.

> **MAKE A *CHOICE* TO BE WILLING TO FIND THE JOY.**

A NICE ROUND HEAD

Uncovering Strength

Nothing is more beautiful than the smile
that has struggled through the tears.

DEMI LOVATO

DID I MENTION IT was my husband's birthday—May 17—
when I was diagnosed with Stage 3, triple-negative breast cancer in
2011? It was one heck of a birthday present for poor, sweet Craig.
I called him with the news on a Tuesday afternoon as he sat in a
sand-dusted tent in the Middle East. He was on active duty with
the Navy, a million miles away. We made the difficult decision that

he would finish his tour, and I would go through treatment with the support of my incredible family and friends until he returned in September.

I know some people think that was crazy. But even if Craig had come home, he would have been gone three or four days a week as an airline pilot, and having medical insurance during those times was *vital*. Plus, I really did have an incredible support system at home.

My treatment plan for breast cancer was simple. The doctors and nurses would shoot massive amounts of chemicals into my body on a weekly or biweekly basis that would bring me to the brink of death, then cut off a boob or two, and then top it off with thirty-seven rounds of a good laser-frying through radiation. Two types of chemotherapy, a mastectomy, and radiation that totaled eleven months of treatment. It sounded surprisingly doable and incomprehensible all at the same time.

I had a biopsy on Monday, pathology on Tuesday, scans on Wednesday and Thursday, a port put in on Friday, and then chemotherapy treatments began the following Monday. It was a

TODAY I WEAR THIS SCAR LIKE A BADGE OF HONOR, NEVER TRYING TO HIDE IT OR COVER IT.

whirlwind of crazy emotions and decisions. It was a bit like riding in the car with that friend who slams on the brakes for no obvious reason, then stomps on the gas when the light ahead is clearly red. If you're feeling a little confused and jerked around by my mixed metaphors, then you're starting to understand what that time was like for me.

One day after my diagnosis, I met with a surgeon. He was going to insert the port into my body that would allow me to receive chemotherapy intravenously. It would stay in my body for the next couple of years and leave a small scar on my chest, a line about three-fourths of an inch long. (Today, I wear this scar like a badge of honor, never trying to hide it or cover it.)

I WAS *CERTAIN* THE COST OF THIS JOURNEY WOULD NOT BE JUST MY HAIR AND HEALTH, BUT ALSO MY JOY AND HAPPINESS.

After a detailed discussion on my upcoming surgery, I rose to leave and put my hand on the door. The doctor had one more thing to add. "Hey," he said, "you know you're not going to die from this, right? Women just don't die from this anymore."

In hindsight, it probably wasn't the most accurate thing for a surgeon to say, but I believed him. I never thought I was going to

die. I had this vision in my mind that I would have "a flu" of sorts for a year, but I could manage that. Naive of me, maybe, but it worked. I was able to fight cancer without ever really contemplating my mortality. I would live, and the cancer would most certainly die. So no, my survival wasn't in question.

But I was *certain* the cost of this journey would not be just my hair and health, but also my joy and happiness. During my first week of diagnosis, a woman I didn't know told me this would be "the best and worst year of your life," and I was pretty sure she was only half right—there was going to be no "best" about it.

Turns out, she *was* only half right. I can now say, unequivocally, it was not the worst. Some of the sweetest gifts and most precious moments of joy in my life came out of my year of cancer, and I am so grateful for them.

Finding joy and laughter in the smallest of moments is critical. Did it suck to be diagnosed? Yep. Was I mad? Of course. Was I scared? Absolutely. But there was joy and even belly-hugging laughter through all of it.

One of the least likely places I found joy was with the loss of my hair. For me, losing my hair was devastating. I wrapped so much of my identity into having "good hair." I could not fathom being without it.

When the first round of chemo was upon me, the instructions

and details were many, but all I wanted to know in that moment was: *When would I start to lose my hair?* My oncologist confidently told me seventeen to nineteen days after the first treatment. He lied.

I was fourteen days out from my first chemo treatment. My sister Jodie was about to arrive from Houston to care for me during my next round of chemo, which would happen the next day. I was excited to see her, and I was feeling pretty good. I got dressed, put on my makeup, and went into the bathroom to style my new short hair.

When I was first diagnosed, I quickly made the decision to cut my hair. I thought it would be less of a shock for my four-year-old, Ella, to see it go from long to short rather than long hair to no hair (it wasn't).

I squirted styling cream into my hands, rubbed them together, and ran my fingers through my hair. As I pulled my hands down, I saw that they were filled with hair. Every time I touched my head, hair was coming out in my fingers. It just kept coming out. This couldn't be happening.

I WASN'T READY FOR THIS.

I don't know what I thought it would look like, how I thought it would all happen, but I don't believe anything in the world could have prepared me for that moment.

This was day fourteen, and my doctor had said days seventeen to nineteen. Panic flooded my body, and the tears wouldn't stop. I wasn't ready for this. I wasn't ready to lose my hair and look like a woman with cancer. *Please, God,* I prayed, *don't let this be happening. Please make it stop, please, not now. I'm not ready.*

Jodie's flight was landing in an hour. It took everything in me to stop this emotional tidal wave and pick her up. I arrived at the airport, and there she was, standing on the curb with her big, beautiful smile. I got out, and the moment our eyes met, the tears began pouring down both our faces. My sister got to the car and wrapped her arms around me. I whispered into her neck, "My hair is falling out. It's not supposed to happen yet, but it's all coming out." We just stood, wrapped in each other's arms as the world went on around us, crying over the loss of my hair.

Eventually, Jodie pulled away, looked in my eyes, and said, "It's going to be okay. We've got this. Do you want to shave it?"

I realized I did want to shave it. I couldn't imagine hair all over my pillows, my clothes, my house. I needed it off.

"Okay, let's do this," she said. "We're going to need some sharp scissors, a razor, and some really good music."

It was one of the hardest things I have ever done—and I suspect it was for Jodie too—but we pushed aside everything we believed about the importance of hair and embraced the task.

First, she shaved the back and carved my initials into my buzzed head. We took pictures and laughed. Next, she shaped my hair into a spiked mohawk and took more photos of her shaving artistry. We were laughing; we were crying—tears of joy inextricably mixed with tears of fear, anger, and sadness.

A few more passes with the razor, and then she handed me the mirror.

Where my long, flowing hair had grown full and lush for forty-one years, there was a smooth, white head. No color, no sun-kissed skin, just white. This was the mark of cancer, the chemo head, and I couldn't deny it any longer. I felt ugly, my head was cold, and I was humiliated. I hated it, and my tears wouldn't stop.

During this time, Craig and I spoke daily over Skype. He was so far away, but he did such a good job at staying connected to me. Two hours after the shaving incident, Craig was scheduled to call from Bahrain. How could I let my husband see me? I felt like every bit of my feminin-ity was gone. What man would ever want to be with a woman who looked like this?

I was terrified to see his face, to see the look of

"OH MY GOSH," HE SAID, "YOU LOOK SO BEAUTIFUL. YOU REALLY DO. YOU LOOK SO BEAUTIFUL."

pity and maybe even disgust in his eyes. I was so embarrassed to see him. I wanted to hide.

The computer rang, and with fear and dread, I connected our screens. Craig's screen came into focus, and I saw his face appear before me. I was bracing for his look of shock and pity.

But instead, I watched his face light up, his eyes widen, and a smile spread across his mouth. All I could see were joy and love in his eyes. "Oh my gosh," he said, "you look so beautiful. You really do. You look so beautiful."

My eyes filled with tears as I pulled my hands to my head, trying to cover the bald ugliness. He told me to put my hands down, that I was beautiful. I don't think Craig Barton has ever looked at me with more love than he did in that very moment.

I COULDN'T HAVE HAD THAT MOMENT WITH MY HUSBAND HAD WE NOT EXPERIENCED THE PAIN OF CANCER FROM WHICH IT WAS BIRTHED.

It will forever be one of the most precious, unforgettable moments I have ever had with my husband—or in my entire life. I remember it like it was yesterday. I see his face so clearly, even now, every detail of that call. It was a moment filled with so much joy and love, and now I know I couldn't have had that moment with my husband had we not experienced the pain of cancer from which it was birthed.

Sometimes my journey of cancer felt like a million years long. I was so sick, so worn down, so exhausted, and some days I wondered if I would ever pull through. The feelings are still raw, and emotions are still right there at the surface, even six years later. But I am in awe that God can give such incredible moments of joy in the most painful of circumstances.

When life hurts and pain is a constant, it is difficult to find—

> **WITHOUT THE REALLY HARD MOMENTS, THE WONDERFUL ONES CAN'T STAND OUT SO VIVIDLY.**

let alone recognize—joy. But without the really hard moments, the wonderful ones can't stand out so vividly. They go hand in hand. Our hard times are blessings too. It might not feel like it at the time, but when you look back, you can see how God was orchestrating your moments to be a part of who you are—your story, your message, and your gift to others.

It's up to us to look for the joy, but it's always there, even in a bald head.

The next day Jodie and I went to the hospital for another round of chemo. After my treatment, we headed across the street to a large department store to look for scarves for my head. I had only one scarf, and it was ugly. I wanted something more fashionable (if there even was such a thing).

As I stood and looked through the scarves, I saw a gorgeous silk one with soft, beautiful colors. I wanted to see how it would look against my bald, white head, so I pulled off my own scarf. In that instant, I noticed another woman browsing right by me—she had seen me remove my scarf, revealing my bald head. My eyes met hers, and I had an immediate feeling of embarrassment.

"Oh my gosh, I'm so sorry," I said quickly, as if I had done something dreadfully wrong in showing my scalp. She stopped, looked at me dead in the eyes, and said, "Oh, honey, I've been there. Don't you ever apologize for being a fighter. You are beautiful."

Tears filled my eyes, and she walked away. She was one of the sweetest gifts of my cancer journey. I never felt the need to cover my head again.

There in the store, I didn't know what kind of suffering that woman had been through. I didn't know what it was like for her to have "been there." But her message of strength was a gift to me. Like my husband's words of love were a gift to me. Good things kept happening when I stopped covering up. I think if we wear our scars, our stories, our bald heads proudly, moments of joy rise to find us.

THE JOY IN GETTING LUCKY

Celebrating the Little Wins

He reached down from on high and took hold
of me; he drew me out of deep waters.

2 SAMUEL 22:17

IF YOU'RE GOING TO schedule a day to have your boob cut off, you really can't go wrong with 11/11/11. It's a day that will live in infamy, and it gives me the opportunity to use the word *infamy* on a regular basis. This easy-to-remember date also helps me walk into any doctor's office and fill out my medical history with ease. Little wins became a *big* deal in my cancer journey, and they still are today.

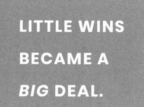

LITTLE WINS BECAME A *BIG* DEAL.

But this story is less about cutting off a boob and more about developing a relationship—with a prosthetic breast I affectionately named "Lucky."

Let me give you a little backstory on Lucky.

In October, while I was in the throes of chemo, I flew to MD Anderson in Houston for a mastectomy consultation. If I was going to have anything chopped off my body, I wanted the people with knives to be boob-chopping every day, not once or twice a year.

In my mind, I imagined I would arrive, they would give me the whole once-over, and I would pick a date for a double mastectomy. On this same scheduled date, they would put in some implants, and I'd emerge from the hospital with the most beautiful, post-cancer breasts ever. I would wear tube tops every day in celebration. It was a dream come true out of a nightmare circumstance, and I was ready.

But my vision of breast perfection did not come to fruition. My surgeon informed me that in situations like mine, they do not take

both breasts. Turns out, your chances of complications from the mastectomy are higher than the chances of the cancer recurring in the other breast. And to make things even more fun, I was not a candidate for implants because of the amount of radiation I would be receiving.

To top off the whole miserable appointment, the doctor told me I had to wait at least a year to have reconstructive surgery.

I was mad—I mean, *really* mad. I had these huge breasts and one was going to be cut off and one was staying. To say I would be lopsided would be a massive understatement. I argued. I fought. I cried. But medical wisdom won, and I had the single mastectomy.

Having a mastectomy on my right breast does not rank high on the list of my favorite moments. Flat as a board on the right, saggy as an eighty-year-old granny on the left. I was branded with a ten-inch scar from the middle of my chest to under my arm. It traced where a breast once was, and now all that remained was skin resting on bone. The surgeons scraped away every bit of tissue, making certain no traces of cancer had been left. Looking in the mirror would never be the same. I was devastated at the sight.

Enter Lucky. Prior to Lucky, it had never occurred to me that prosthetic breasts existed. I'd always known about prosthetics for arms or legs, but I'd never, ever thought about a prosthetic breast.

I guess I assumed I'd just shove a few pairs of socks in my bra or something—until, that is, my doctor gave me a prescription for a breast prosthetic. Yes, you can actually get a script for that . . . like an antibiotic for flatness.

Shopping for a boob is both comical and eye-opening. Some things I didn't know before embarking on this particular shopping spree:

- A prosthetic boob has to weigh a good amount to hold your bra down. (Lucky weighed four pounds. Yes, I took him out every time I had to weigh in for something.)
- It feels like a real breast, but it's a triangular shape (not sure why I thought it would look like a ball).
- It's soft and squishy.
- It's topped with a little nubby nipple that sticks out.
- Oh, and super important: you've got to try to find one that resembles your other breast.

We tried lots of prosthetics, searching for the perfect fit. Then I met Lucky. Just the right size and weight. He was a perfect fit in my bra. He matched the rest of me. I strapped him on and was whole again—two breasts and ready to conquer the world!

I didn't know when we met that his name would be Lucky, but after a very comprehensive and well-thought-out Facebook poll, the decision was made. A determining factor in the decision was that every day I wore it, I could say I was "gettin' Lucky." I know, childishly bad, but it made me laugh. And I needed laughter. Plus, if you haven't picked up on it by now, I never pass up an opportunity for a little bit of levity.

> **NEVER PASS UP AN OPPORTUNITY TO INJECT SOME LEVITY.**

Lucky was fabulous. We went everywhere together, and like most new relationships, everything was beautiful in the beginning. I was so appreciative of Lucky; I took such good care of him. But then the euphoria of newness began to wear off, and I started to notice things I did not like so much about Lucky.

Lucky was oh-so-*hot*. Lucky was a rubbery, four-pound mass stuck to my chest. He was sweaty and sticky. (In Lucky's defense, he did come with two soft cotton covers, but I managed to misplace them both within the first two weeks.)

So I started trying to ditch Lucky. Often. Trips to restaurants always included secret dashes to the restroom to take out Lucky and hide him in my purse. He would frequently end up riding in the passenger seat of my car between destinations. I didn't wear him until I absolutely needed to.

Within seconds of walking in the door at home, Lucky would get thrown on the sofa. Like unzipping those tight jeans or taking off an uncomfortable bra, Lucky was *out*. I misplaced Lucky continually. "Has anyone seen my boob?" was a common question around the house.

Dressing became difficult and frustrating. V-neck shirts were hard because, invariably, Lucky would work his way up and peak out. Every. Single. Time. Thankfully, I had a handful of staple pieces that worked, and I even found a swimsuit that disguised my prosthetic perfectly.

Life with Lucky was bearable, at best. That is, until the Hembrees came to visit.

The Hembrees—including my bestie, Casie, her husband, John, and their three kids, Anderson, Carson, and Katelyn—are awesome. They are one of those families that is a perfect match for ours. We like them, and they like us. Casie and I are the dearest of friends, John and Craig have guy things in common, and all the kids get along. This is a rare, wonderful thing.

Every year we enjoy several days of boating and beaching together. This particular year, the Summer of Lucky, we rented a large sailboat in July. We were anchored for the day, waiting for the

> **THIS IS A RARE, WONDERFUL THING.**

incredible Blue Angels to give us an air show. We spent the day laughing and frolicking in the water. Yes, *frolicking*. How often does a person get to use that word and *really* mean it?

Casie and I are cool, fun moms (we think so, anyway). And on this particular afternoon, we decided we were going to jump off the boat and into the water. From our perch near the ladder to the surface of the water below, it was a good eighty-nine feet. Or maybe a little less—maybe like ten feet. Regardless, it felt really high. We were daredevils and about to show the youngsters what it was like to dance with danger. We sat the four children in a perfect row along the edge of the boat so that they could have a prime view of our parental awesomeness.

John was instructed to film every second of it; we needed proof to show generations to come. Casie and I were fearless and ready. We smiled at each other and counted, "One . . . two . . . three . . ." And we jumped! Screaming like banshees, with legs and arms flailing all the way down, Casie and I (and Lucky) plunged into the water.

The moment I hit the surface, I felt Lucky slide out of my swimsuit. The lower he sank into the water, the more thoughts raced through my head. *My boob! Where did my boob go?!* I opened my eyes underwater, searching. *I can't lose Lucky! Will insurance cover another one? Oh my gosh, I love Lucky! I NEED Lucky. I am not whole without Lucky. Lucky, where are you?!*

But the water was far too deep and dark to find him.

My head popped out of the water, and I looked right at John, who had his camera in hand and was still filming. I yelled to him, "I lost Lucky!"

For a brief moment, we looked at each other. Dumbfounded. Then, suddenly, about fifteen feet away, we watched Lucky burst victoriously out of the water. It was like a torpedo darting up from the depths of the sea.

I was elated. "My boob!" I yelled, and I began swimming to it. Prior to this incident, I had no idea Lucky knew how to float.

I also had no idea the children were watching every single second of this unfold. The little row of four- and six-year-olds sat perfectly still, their eyes wide and their jaws resting on their laps. *How on earth will I explain that my breast just came bursting forth from the water to these innocent children?*

CHANCES ARE I SCARRED THE CHILDREN FOR LIFE, BUT IT WAS WORTH IT.

John Hembree, filming it all, was laughing so hard he could not speak.

Chances are I scarred the children for life, but it was worth it. I laughed so hard tears were streaming down my face. I couldn't catch my breath, and neither could Casie. It was a fabulously hilarious moment, and it's a story we tell over and over. *Remember when Mrs. Dawn's boob shot out of the water?* And, of course, the video gets pulled out about fifty times a year.

And why wouldn't we tell that story over and over? It's certainly as good as *Free Willy.* And Lucky has at least as much star quality as Wilson from *Castaway.* So I'll take it. There have been a lot of little wins in this story of girl meets boob, and I'll take them all—from the moment we met to his dramatic near-death experience. I'll pump them up and celebrate them like we're in *Rocky* and we just made it to the top of the stairs. All the little wins—I'm going to go ahead and call them epic wins. Movie-worthy wins. And I'll delight in them all. Because in times like these, each little win is worth replaying over and over again.

Adding 2 Samuel 22:17 at the start of this chapter was a little cheeky Bible humor for you.

YOU GET TO

Learning to Treasure What You Didn't Want

Now eagerly desire the greater gifts. And yet
I will show you the most excellent way.

1 CORINTHIANS 12:31

A DEEP BREATH AND a huge, slow eye roll. That was my immediate reaction. A family member had just said to me, "You *get* to."

This was her attempt at reminding me of the holiest of postures—gratitude—so I'd do something I absolutely did not want to do: clean my child's vomit off my dress and new suede shoes. I can assure you there was no feeling of gratitude in this moment as I stood covered in vomit at my cousin's wedding.

"Honey, you *get to* clean that vomit."

You get to.

If you're not familiar with this worldview, it's an idea espoused by pretty much every pastor, women's conference speaker, and all-knowing aunt I've ever encountered: to truly enjoy life the way God wants us to, we must be grateful 24-7. We should be grateful for the little things, the big things, the smelly things, the happy and the sad—in all things we should be grateful.

The truth is this: that annoying family member was right. And I do believe it now.

Finding joy in the messy, tedious tasks of our everyday lives is darn near impossible sometimes. Driving the kids to school, going to your job, helping with homework, keeping up with sports, meals, and exercise, feeling miserable about what you just ate, and wearing an underwire bra when all you want to do is let those puppies loose—every single day, life is hard, ladies. I know. The tasks seem never-ending, and it can be so difficult to find joy in the tedium.

Until one day, when everything that makes your eyes roll is taken away.

EVERY SINGLE DAY LIFE IS HARD, LADIES. I KNOW.

Overnight those tasks and routines can become the precious little places where joy is birthed. The struggle quickly becomes the gift.

My youngest daughter, Ellason, was four years old when I was diagnosed with breast cancer, and Makenzie, my oldest, was married and out of the house, tending to her own family about an hour away. My husband, Craig, was in a dusty tent in the Middle East. It was just Ellason and me at home, with a lot of love and support from family and friends.

> **OVERNIGHT THOSE TASKS AND ROUTINES CAN BECOME THE PRECIOUS LITTLE PLACES WHERE JOY IS BIRTHED.**

During the biopsy on my right breast, something went wrong, and they burned the skin, leaving a half-inch, black, circular burn at the incision point. Believe it or not, that burn turned out to be one of the best things to happen to me. That burn became something visible and tangible I could use to explain cancer to a four-year-old little girl. We called it the "booby bug," and it made sense to her sweet four-year-old mind. The booby bug made mommy sick.

Getting rid of the booby bug was a lot harder than I imagined it would be.

Chemotherapy was a wild beast, and it kicked my butt. The plan was six rounds of a chemo combination called "red devil" (because one of the drugs was red in color), and I would receive those treatments every two weeks. The next phase was a different type of drug that I would receive weekly for twelve weeks, totaling six months of chemotherapy treatments.

My chemo weeks looked a little like this:

Day 1: Chemo infusion. A nurse covered in protective gear—large plastic mask and all—inserted IVs into the port in my chest and changed them every hour until my body was filled with what I like to call "the poison drugs."

(Side note: Someone should give you a heads-up that your nurse is going to look like the hazmat dudes in *ET* when she walks in to give you chemotherapy drugs. That image sort of shakes you up. I mean, if the nurse is covered three ways to Sunday so she won't touch the drugs, why is it a good idea to put them *inside* of my body? Food for thought.)

The entire process lasted about four hours, and then someone would drive me home. Off to bed I would go, feeling tired but otherwise alive.

Day 2: The poison drugs hit. Nausea meds and painkillers were a must, but this wasn't the worst part. The worst part was that I had to go back to the cancer center for a bone marrow stimulant injection that increased my white blood cell count so my body could fight infection.

I hated it. Imagine feeling so nauseated, with pain seething through every inch of your body, and knowing you have to go back to get a shot that'll make you feel substantially worse. From a mental perspective, Day 2 was always the hardest for me.

Days 3–4: The crescendo of suffering. The poison drugs battled with my body. They were pure misery. I prayed, cried, and begged for God's mercy through them.

Day 5: A hint of hope. A small flicker of light appeared at the end of the tunnel, and I began to feel *a bit* of relief from the process.

The first five days are followed by nine days of recovery and desperately reaching for normalcy until the cycle ends and I am shoved back to the starting line all over again for the next Day 1.

The more rounds of chemo I had, the longer the miserable part of the process would take. The effects of Day 2 would stretch over two or three days. And the effects of Days 3 and 4—my rock-bottom days—would sometimes last almost a week. The overwhelming pain, nausea, and discomfort were constant, and so were my pleading prayers.

But I can't write honestly about my chemo days without adding this: it was in the agony and sickness that I found God on the most beautiful and intimate level. Nothing has pried open my raw, aching heart like having my body and soul assailed by that disease and its horrific treatment. In the depths of my pain, I came to know Him best. I believe it is often at our most helpless, our most vulnerable, that we are most primed to hear and see Him.

Anyway, back to the vomit at my cousin's wedding. Yes, it all comes full circle.

I'm sharing the not-so-pleasant details of my chemo routine to paint a picture of what life was like in that season, but also to give you some background on how I learned to embrace the "you get to" philosophy.

While I was undergoing treatment, there was no driving Ella to school, no making her lunches or picking out her clothes. There was no playtime, no homework together, no running and tickling.

I wanted to play an active role in my own life, and I couldn't. Chemo was a prize-fighting boxer, and I was on the ground slamming my hands against the floor to tap out. I wanted to be done; I begged for it to be over. I wanted to be a mom, and I didn't want to be sick a moment longer.

Despite how hard I was fighting, I was still riddled with guilt over the kind of mother I was to Ella. I think women are the only creatures who can be gripping the ring of a toilet in sickness and still feeling guilty that they can't drive their babies to school. We are crazy, beautiful creatures, aren't we?

As I fought through weeks of chemo, I found moments of joy and laughter with Ella. Not on a playground or in a car drive, but in the sweet, quiet moments lying in my bed with her snuggled next to me, close to my belly and wrapped in my arms.

I am not sure if I comforted her more or if she comforted me, but Ellason was my saving grace at the end of each day. When I felt well enough, I would make up stories, starring her as the princess, me as the queen, and daddy as the king. (The queen was always very beautiful, of course.) The stories would change daily, and she loved it.

After months of treatment, I remember the day I was finally able to pick up Ellason from school. I was elated that I'd been given a two-week break from chemo, and I finally felt well enough to drive. It was something so small, but it meant so much. When the normal, everyday pieces of life get taken away, you realize they make up a beautiful and wonderful existence.

Before cancer, I had taken so

FIGHT FOR MOMENTS OF JOY AND HOPE. ALL THESE THINGS— YOU *GET TO* DO THEM.

much of this for granted; I even thought of some of those activities as the burdens. (*What do you mean, you need lunch again? Didn't we just do that yesterday?*) In reality, these mundane activities were the sweet blessings of life. When cancer took away the mundane, I finally understood driving my daughter to school was a gift.

Chemo was teaching me how to fight for moments of joy and hope. I was learning to look for them, and I was realizing all those things I resented were actually things I *got* to do. In fact, I eventually reached a rather revolutionary level of "you get to" mastery.

Remember what Days 1 through 5 looked like during my chemo treatments? The beast of chemo was destroying me and my life; I hated the treatments and all that came with them. I hated walking into that cancer center and being poisoned each time. Chemo was the enemy—that is, until I learned my hardest "you get to" lesson.

Every time I arrived to get chemo, nurses took my vitals and drew my blood to make sure I was "healthy enough" to be poisoned. My body was weaker each round, and my white blood cell count needed to be more than one thousand. When I walked in for my fourth round of red devil, I was fighting with all that I had—but this time I was also battling a fever.

HOW COULD I WANT SOMETHING I SO INTENSELY LOATHED?

After a few minutes, the nurse walked over and with pity in her eyes said, "I'm so sorry. We can't give you chemo. Your white count is too low." My body wouldn't be able to fight the infection.

I actually *couldn't* get the thing I hated getting most. This was the beginning of a big mind-shift for me. At first I was a little relieved. They gave me a shot of white blood cell booster, hoping to increase my white count overnight, and sent me home.

The next day I arrived, and I was ready. My vitals were taken, blood was drawn, and soon I would be heading back for the red devil.

But wait. "Dawn," the nurse said, "your counts are too low again. I am so sorry. We will try again tomorrow."

The tears fell so fast and so hard and wouldn't stop for hours. I needed this chemo to fight cancer; I had to have it. How could I want something I so intensely loathed?

That's when I realized: I needed to change the story in my head. Chemo was a gift. I *get to* get chemo.

Chemo gave me the ability to fight cancer and live. It was a gift that generations before me did not have.

Three days later I was able to receive my gift again.

I would love to tell you that my view on

I NEEDED TO CHANGE THE STORY IN MY HEAD.

making lunches and driving to school has remained in a place of gratitude, that I do it daily with a skip in my step and joy in my heart, but I would be lying. I am human.

I complain. I get overwhelmed and annoyed. I grow tired of driving back and forth to school. I roll my eyes at a busy schedule. I loathe going to the grocery store.

But I do have a gift that many don't. When it all seems like too much, I have the gift of remembering what it felt like to have it all taken away. I remember what it felt like to desperately want to drive a little girl to school and go to a playground with her. I know that feeling, and I am grateful for it. I *get to* make those lunches. I *get to* clean her vomit off my shoes.

> WHEN IT ALL SEEMS LIKE TOO MUCH, I HAVE THE GIFT OF REMEMBERING WHAT IT FELT LIKE TO HAVE IT ALL TAKEN AWAY.

Never in a million years would I have dreamed the diagnosis of cancer was a gift. But I can tell you unequivocally it was. A crazy, wild, precious gift. I *got to* battle cancer. In that battle I learned to love my family more, and I met God on a whole new level. So whether it's a life-changing battle or one of those mildly irritating or gross parts of life, they don't look so bad when that story in your head changes. When you realize that the gifts you're being given are right there in that unattractive packaging. You *get to* open them, and you might find out that God designed them just for you—for your good and His glory.

SHE'S STILL
YOUR FRIEND

Loving People Where They Are

A friend is one who knows you as you are, understands
where you have been, accepts what you have
become, and still, gently allows you to grow.

"THIS ILLNESS HAS SHOWN me who my *real* friends
are." Sound familiar? If you ever post something like this, chances
are pretty good that I will come and pull your hair and possibly
break your pinky fingernails.

Totally kidding. I won't do that. But I will dramatically roll my eyes at you like a teenager.

I'm here to speak in defense of the friends who don't show up when you're sick. The ones you might see regularly at dance class and school pickup and the grocery store and the gym (okay, maybe at the ice cream store next to the gym). The ones you've come to consider as friends because they're in your social circle or your daily orbit in a number of ways—and then, suddenly, you're sick in bed and they're no longer in your daily orbit.

Listen—friendship is not defined by how often a friend takes you to a doctor's appointment or cooks dinner for you. Sorry, but it's true.

LIFE IS NOT A GAME OF KEEPING TALLY MARKS ON WHO DID MORE FOR US DURING SEASONS OF HURT.

Just because a friend lacks the gift of caring for the sick doesn't mean she doesn't love you. It doesn't mean she's not a true friend for life. And you know what else? Just because a friend *does* have the gift of caring for the sick doesn't necessarily mean she's a friend for life.

Life is not a game of keeping tally marks on who did more for us during seasons of hurt. It's about seeing the beautiful through the pain, about noticing the unexpected gifts God puts in our lives in the hard times.

Take the season my baby started preschool. On her first day I spent about sixty seconds celebrating my newfound freedom before curling up on the floor in a fetal position, knowing that my last child was going off to school. This was the end of an era for me, and I was sad. Luckily, that sadness lasted for about five minutes—because that's when Kimi Steinberg pulled up in her minivan.

I want you to visualize the most stunning female you have ever seen in a little five-foot-two body. Now imagine a baby bump on the front of that gorgeous body sticking out two, maybe three, feet.

She was a massively pregnant specimen of physical perfection, and I grew to adore everything about her. She was honest, kind, real, and joy radiated from her. She was a tiny woman with the mouth of a drunken sailor. I loved her.

Kimi was a former oncology nurse at the Mayo Clinic and had moved to town recently with her husband, two kids, and a baby on the way. Our daughters became inseparable best friends, and Kimi and I spent countless hours together—which was terrific because Craig was deployed to Bahrain and Kimi's husband was a physician who worked long hours. "Single mommin' it" together was a lot more fun.

The months passed and our friendship continued to blossom. Then in May, there was a lump in my breast, a biopsy, and a diagnosis of Stage 3 breast cancer. Kimi was on deck. The woman God put in my life to go through this journey with me was a spectacular little oncology nurse.

She went to my appointments with me, she took notes, and she even translated the language of medical terminology into English. As I tried to process everything, she held me during my emotional breakdowns, and she still managed to make me laugh. She understood that, through all of this, we needed to laugh.

SOMETIMES GOD PUTS PEOPLE IN YOUR LIFE JUST FOR A SEASON OR A REASON.

And then she was gone. She was a gift from God during that season, but within twenty-four months, she moved away to Iowa. I will forever love and treasure her, but today we speak only sparingly in the craziness of our lives.

Sometimes God puts people in your life just for a season or a reason. Other times they are there for a lifetime. And both are precious and perfect forms of friendship. I look back and wonder, *What are the chances I would randomly meet this wonderful, tiny pregnant woman, that she would be an oncology nurse, and that I would be diagnosed with cancer several months into our friendship?* None. God planted this sweet friendship in my life. It was a beautiful gift.

Of course, Kimi wasn't the only one propping me up while I battled cancer when Craig was in Bahrain. It was all happening so fast; it was overwhelming and so hard to understand. Many days I struggled to keep water down, let alone take care of a home and a child. Thankfully, other angels came into my life. I had so many people helping me navigate this season.

People sent cards, dropped off meals, cleaned the house, took Ella to school and playdates, and so much more. I was covered in love and support from my friends, my company, my church, and my community. It was as if God wrapped me in a blanket of love to keep me warm while Craig was gone.

Not all of these people were "friends"—some I barely knew. Many were people who had the gift of caring for others in need, and they serve by helping those who cannot care for themselves.

> THEY SHINE WHEN THEY ARE ABLE TO GIVE OF THEMSELVES AND MAKE OTHERS FEEL BETTER.

It is part of their calling, and they shine when they are able to give of themselves and make others feel better.

Many of those people who swooped into my life during this time swooped out once I was well. Not because they didn't care, but because their gifts of helping, serving, and tending were no longer needed.

This gift of serving and caring for others is a beautiful gift to have, but not everybody has it. I do not, and neither does one of my best friends, Kali.

During my months of cancer, I rarely saw Kali. She did not go to chemo with me, or bring food, or care for Ella. She called often, and we laughed. She stayed with me emotionally, but the girl wasn't cooking any meals or cleaning my toilets.

It wasn't because Kali didn't love me or didn't care. I knew she did. It was because those things are just not Kali. But she showed me love in her own way, and in the summer of 2011, she hit it out of the park.

I was two months into the chemo journey, and I was miserable and sick. It was July, which meant it was time for my company's annual seminar in Dallas. The Mary Kay Cosmetics Seminar was the ultimate celebration of our achievements, complete with evening gowns and pageantry. I loved this event, and I'd never missed one in four years of being part of Mary Kay. But I was going to have to miss it this time.

Enter Kali Brigham. If I couldn't go to Seminar, she was bringing Seminar to me.

Kali arrived at my door with flowers, sashes, and diamonds—everything a girl would need for a big awards show. She topped it off with a little crown for me to wear, made from her daughter's stretchy headband and a miniature tiara. She knew me and understood how important that event was to me.

Kali didn't love me less because she didn't bring over meals, help clean my house, or care for Ella. Would she have done these if I had asked? Absolutely. But I knew she didn't have the gift of nurturing the sick. She has many other gifts I am blessed with almost daily.

Okay, I can hear you asking, "But what about the ones who *really* don't show up?"

Because, yes, Kali called me regularly, and she showed up big-time for my personal Seminar extravaganza. What about the women I didn't see or hear from during the awfulness of my cancer treatment? Are they still real friends?

The answer is *yes.*

I want you to know this: when you go through a difficult time, a person you love may not behave the way you expect or hope, but this doesn't mean they do not love you deeply. Some people don't know how to care for those who are ill, or

> **WHEN YOU GO THROUGH A DIFFICULT TIME, A PERSON YOU LOVE MAY NOT BEHAVE THE WAY YOU EXPECT OR HOPE, BUT THIS DOESN'T MEAN THEY DO NOT LOVE YOU DEEPLY.**

they simply don't *want* to care for those who are ill. People show love in different ways. Sometimes people just don't know what to say, so they say nothing.

And that is okay. Give them grace.

Sometimes your seasons are badly timed. Just when you are at your neediest, your friend may be channeling all she's got toward her own needs. Maybe it's a new baby, a demanding job, a sick parent, a rocky relationship, a difficult teenager—the list goes on and on and on. Maybe she keeps meaning to check on you, or maybe you fell off her radar completely for a while.

> PEOPLE SHOW LOVE IN DIFFERENT WAYS. AND THAT IS OKAY. GIVE THEM GRACE.

That is okay too. Give her grace.

The women who came to my house to care for me didn't love me more than any of my other friends, and my friends who didn't come didn't love me less. It was simply a season when each person was showing love the best way she knew how.

Be grateful God puts nurturing people in your life during those seasons of sickness or hurt or pain. Those friends and strangers are functioning in their strengths. We must embrace people for the gifts they have during the seasons they show them and quit judging—or giving up on—people who don't have the gift we're looking for at a particular time.

I'm actually a lot like Kali in this arena. As I mentioned, my strengths do not include nurturing and helping others when they are sick—even now, after having been through the hell that is cancer treatment. If you are sick, I probably won't be the friend to bring you dinner, clean your house, or take care of your kids. It simply is not who I am. I will call or come by and try to make you laugh a little, or I'll arrange to have pizza delivered—because that's how I show love.

Maybe your hardship will come in a season when my life is hit by its own little tidal wave, in which case I might become that didn't-show-up friend who needs your grace.

Love people where they are, even when your world is falling apart.

WE MUST EMBRACE PEOPLE FOR THE GIFTS THEY HAVE DURING THE SEASONS THEY SHOW THEM.

Give grace because we really don't know what is going on behind closed doors. And for the love of Pete, do not plaster things like "Now I know who my *real* friends are" across social media. Don't give up. Don't despair. You've got a complex life, blessed with the gift of many types of people who are living their own complex lives. Why would you toss that gift aside? They still love you. Let it go, girl.

LOVE PEOPLE WHERE
THEY ARE, EVEN
WHEN YOUR WORLD
IS FALLING APART.

THE JOY IN
EXERCISING

What Doesn't Kill You Makes You Stronger

Sweat is just fat crying.

I HAVE FOUND NO joy in exercising—don't do it.

Okay, okay, I can't use this book to tell the world that exercise is bad and not to do it. I know—*we all know*—exercising is good for us. But I hate it. I want to love it, and I just can't. I want all the results of a hard-bodied, twenty-five-year-old woman with absolutely none of the work.

Seems reasonable, doesn't it?

There hasn't been a single day in my life when I've looked at my schedule and said to myself, *Oh, hey, I'm gonna feel miserable, and I am going to do it every single day. I'll pencil in my one-hour death torture right here at 8:00 a.m.* That just sounds like bad decision-making and poor time management to me.

I realize not everybody feels the way I do. Two of my closest friends—Kali and Stephanie—love to work out daily. (Yes, like every single day. Weird, I know.) I swear, I have heard them talk about exercise like it's a free shopping spree they *get to* go on. Hard pass.

Last year the company I was working for sent its top achievers on a two-week luxury vacation that started in Vancouver, Canada, and ended with an Alaskan cruise. I had the honor of attending this trip with Kali, Stephanie, and my dear friend Casie, plus a few husbands. Our group fell into two camps: Steph and Kali, crazy workout people. Dawn and Casie, not so much.

Ten days before departing on vacation, I received a very high-energy call from Stephanie. I could tell from the way she screamed my name it was going to be good. Something huge like, "I just won half a million dollars, and I want to spend it on a yacht to cruise the Italian Riviera with you and all of our friends!"

Instead, our conversation took a hard turn down the road of "bad ideas" and "maybe we shouldn't be friends."

"You aren't going to believe this," Stephanie announced. "Vancouver has a SoulCycle!"

"Uh, okay," I said, confused but curious. "Is that a new-age spa that relaxes your soul?"

"No, it's this incredible cycling gym. You are going to love it."

Stop right there, sister. Have we even met? At any point in our relationship have I ever even hinted I think it would be fun to work out on vacation? That my idea of a good time on any given day includes exercise and sweating? I dread it during normal life, and I'm certainly not going to force it into my luxury time.

"I love you, Steph, but I don't think so."

Conversation over. Friendship in question.

Honestly, the whole cycle thing completely baffles me. Just riding a comfy beach cruiser with a big, wide seat hurts my girly parts. Why would I want to do it with half the seat? You want me to pedal as fast as my out-of-shape legs can go to really loud music? (I should add I've just hit the age where I'm saying things like "What's that noise?" and "Oh my gosh, turn that down!" a lot.) And you want me to do this in front of a bunch of *strangers*?

I know how this ends. My girly parts start hurting from the seat, and I can't sit any longer. I try the stand-up pedal move, and my legs give out. Then I'm face-planting on the little dashboard that's flashing a frantic "High Heart Rate!" alert while my feet, trapped by the pedal straps, continue looping round and round. The skinny strangers look on, totally bewildered.

As you can see, nothing about this idea is appealing to me. Nothing. Plus, if I am going to pedal that hard, shouldn't I actually go somewhere?

Yeah, *nahhh*. I'll skip this one.

Though I couldn't understand Steph's excitement about cycling, I do have the same level of excitement about eating. Like, if she had said, "I just got this pill that'll let us eat as much as we want the whole vacation and we won't gain a pound," I would have been right there with her. So maybe in some small way I understand.

Nevertheless, I delicately declined her invitation.

Our time in Vancouver was amazing, and then the day arrived to board our cruise to Alaska. I wasn't worried about being left alone during exercise excursions. I still had Casie, and Kali hadn't hinted she wanted to hit up the gym on the cruise. Poor Stephanie.

We all boarded, we laughed, we started talking about fun plans. We were happy. And then Kali casually began shifting the conversation to dates and times for all of us to meet . . . in the cruise ship's gym. *Wait, what?*

This wasn't vacation Kali after all. This was regular ol' "Let's have fun by working out!" Kali. She was showing her true colors.

The worst part? Everyone—even the husbands—was acting like this was normal.

What happened to my "Meet me at the bar!" or "See you at the restaurant!" or "Let's play Parcheesi on the lido deck" friends? Why were our definitions of vacation so different? How have I spent my life with these women?

No, Kali, I thought to myself, *I will not be spending my time with you in the gym sweating, gasping for air, begging for it all to stop because Fred over there wanted to show us how fun it is to do burpees on a swaying ship. No, ma'am, not this girl. I am vacationing.*

But I nodded and smiled and waited for the conversation to move on. I knew it would be okay; there was always Casie. She and I are one when it comes to opinions on exercise. I knew this girl would be by my side for a rum-punch-and-spa experience any day. We were *not* going to be one of those twisted gym girls whose moral compass of correct vacation behavior was so clearly warped.

I WAS BEING CALLED TO REEVALUATE ONE OF TWO THINGS: MY CLOSEST FRIENDSHIPS OR MY OWN THINKING ABOUT EXERCISE.

Oh, but she did it. She turned on me. Casie crumbled to exercise peer pressure. It happened so quickly.

All it took was Stephanie's husband, Mike, another workout guru (no, this insane behavior is not limited to the women), telling Casie he could teach her some arm moves. *Bam.* I lost her. Now, with the promise of her own chiseled biceps, she was gone and her knife of betrayal twisted in my back. She was one of them. I was alone.

It started becoming clear to me on this trip that I was being called to reevaluate one of two things: my closest friendships or my own thinking about exercise. I, of course, turned the microscope on my friends first. Who were these women? Did I want to do life with women who found *joy* in exercise? Could I trust them? Who were they *really*?

After a few hours of deep soul-searching, I concluded just because something brings your friends joy but does not bring *you* joy, it doesn't mean you can't be friends with them. Okay, friendship saved.

Then, after many hours of even deeper soul-searching, I hit

MAYBE IT MAKES SENSE TO DIG INTO SOMETHING REALLY HORRIBLE LIKE EXERCISE AND *TRY* TO FIND JOY IN IT. I SAID *MAYBE*.

a new conclusion: Maybe, and I mean *maybe*, they had it right. Maybe it makes sense to dig into something really horrible like exercise and *try* to find joy in it. I said *maybe*.

It was time to find my exercise joy solution. After the cruise, of course.

My solution needed to be a good one, and it came to me in the form of Chip Holston.

Chip owns a local gym called Chip's Gym (I have no doubt it took him countless hours to come up with this name). Two years before my cruise revelation, I had joined Chip's Gym for the first time. I went approximately three times and then, miraculously, my schedule became incredibly full and I became too important and too busy to possibly exercise.

But not to worry, I continued to send my membership fee each month. It was my own personal charity work—you know, support-ing a local business. There was really no need to go; the joy was in sending that monthly check and knowing one more entrepreneur was thriving. You're welcome, local community.

After about a year I stopped supporting that particular local business. Then a few months ago—in the midst of the search for my exercise joy solution—I saw Chip and his wife, Nancy, at church. It sparked an idea: Chip could train me to physical greatness.

Chip is a super-duper weightlifting master, world champion, *and* former Olympic bobsledder (this is a little ironic, given that we live in Florida). Should I have the desire to exercise *or* become an Olympic champion, I was covered. Either way, he was an excellent choice.

Membership signed once again. This time I wasn't going to be trapped into writing that check each month. Oh no, I was set up to pay *annually*. This time I was all in!

Our workout days were set, and this was *it*. I was on my way to being fit-tastic.

We made a schedule to work out a few days a week. And when I say *we*, I mean *me*. Chip has it easy; he just points, counts, and adds weights to things. I'll admit, I quickly started to enjoy my time at the gym—not really the *exercise*, but all that in-between social time with Chip and the other people there. Yes, I now have "gym friends."

But I still wanted to find joy in exercise itself. What I needed was something to get my competitive juices flowing. Being competitive can be a huge motivator for me.

So one morning, to get my mind in the zone, I began imagining the people in the gym were my USA Olympic team cheering section. Don't laugh, it works. Well, you can laugh, but you should try it. Have your friends make cheering sounds quietly in the background while you do something, anything: on the elliptical, lifting free weights, emptying the dishwasher. Seriously, it's fun.

I stepped up to the vertical knee-raise machine. I could hear the announcer as I made my first move. One knee raise . . . and *ahhh, the crowd goes wild! Two knee raises . . . they're on their feet! Can she do it? Can she hit three knee raises?! Why, yes! Yes, she can! Ladies and gentlemen, Dawn Barton brings home the gold once again, and she's set a new world record!*

It was a lot more fun than just counting, "One, two, three." And there's a ton of joy in being a world record–holder in my mind.

Next I decided I would dominate the stair-stepper, and I mean *dominate*. It looked easy enough: walk up the stairs over and over. Got it.

I hit stop on the stair-stepper after fifty-seven minutes. (Fact check: Perceived time was a little off. It was actually closer to seventy-eight seconds.)

Coach yourself, Dawn, I told myself. *You're fine. That was just your body adjusting to the machine. Or maybe you're adjusting to not working out for thirty-seven years. Either way, you've got this. You show this machine who's boss.*

I pressed the start button again and began climbing stairs like a champ. Some 256 minutes (I think) later, my heart rate jumped to 678 beats per minute and my legs were losing the ability to move up and down.

Wait, what? The machine was obviously broken. It said this time I'd only been climbing one minute, fifty-eight seconds.

Due to the machine's inability to accurately track my athletic excellence, I quit using it. I was just too advanced for it. And for the record, walking away from that insidious death trap gave me *a lot* of joy. Back to knee raises and Olympic wins for me.

With time I figured out that one of the best parts of hiring a trainer is this: he gets me there. Every night before my workout, Chip sends me a "See you at 8!" text. I am convinced the majority of what I am paying him for is that text.

> **WHAT ACTUALLY GIVES ME JOY: THE END RESULT.**

That text is the catalyst for what actually gives me joy: the end result. Not the action of the exercise, but the result of it. I feel stronger and less stressed (although being a world champion knee-raiser can be very stressful), I sleep better, and I love the people at the gym.

Endorphins or no endorphins, finding joy in things you don't like is hard. But here's a secret: there is more joy in doing things that are *hard* than doing things that are easy. (The stair-stepper was not hard. It was stupid. There's a difference.)

In other words—and this one is for all of us exercise haters—fit people get *less* joy when they work out than we do because it's *harder* for us; therefore, it's a bigger *win* for us. Bigger win = more joy. Okay, so it's just a theory and possibly a bit of a stretch. (See what I did there?) But I say put that little ditty in your back pocket the next time you strut into the gym, you big, bad, joyful superwoman!

Side note to gym avoiders, Jesus loves all of us the same, and no one is better than anyone else. We are all equal. But Jesus did not go to the gym, so, yes, you are following Him more closely. Pretty sure He would agree.

> THERE IS MORE JOY IN DOING THINGS THAT ARE *HARD* THAN DOING THINGS THAT ARE EASY.

9

MAYBE SHE'S BAD AT MATH?

Looking Beyond Comparison

Let's just go ahead and be what we were made to be,
without enviously or pridefully comparing ourselves
with each other, or trying to be something we aren't.

ROMANS 12:6 MSG

CHISELED, BEAUTIFULLY DEFINED ARMS.
I have prayed for them all my life. They are the ultimate when it
comes to "the unattainable" for me. Instead, I'm blessed with the

arms of a three-hundred-pound sumo wrestler and the neck of a seventy-nine-year-old Tennessee wild turkey.

Through the years, in a small attempt to make myself feel better about these glaring flaws, I have formed a mental fantasy of God creating my body. He's molding me, in all my splendor, bit by bit. But when He gets to my arms, an angel pops in and interrupts. God briefly looks up from what was about to be my elongated, perfect biceps. When He looks back to His work, His eyes go wide and He mutters a quiet, little "oops."

I'm happy to say I have come to accept these physical hiccups and many of my other flaws, because I now understand, on the flip side, I've been given some incredible gifts. Did you catch that? *Some* gifts, not *all* the gifts.

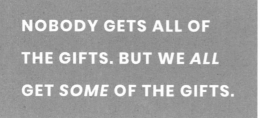

NOBODY GETS ALL OF THE GIFTS. BUT WE *ALL* GET *SOME* OF THE GIFTS.

No one gets *all* the gifts. Well, except Jesus, but that's another story.

I haven't always been so accepting of my flaws. I've reached this point after years of lamenting my own shortcomings and coveting the gifts of other women in my life. I've wasted so much time fixating on the places where friends and strangers were excelling that I almost overlooked my own potential for excellence.

Can you imagine how insulting that was to God? He's all "Why are you looking at her toes? Didn't you see the hands I gave you?"

I get it now. Nobody gets all of the gifts. But we *all* get *some* of the gifts.

> WE FOCUS SO HARD ON WHAT WE DON'T HAVE THAT WE FORGET TO USE WHAT WE DO HAVE.

By my entirely unscientific calculations, there are 1,482 gifts you could end up with. Let's say each human gets 784 of them. That leaves 698 that each person does *not* receive. Here's the problem: we look at the 784 gifts another woman has, and we compare them to the 698 we do not have. This is the root of a troubling disconnect among women: we focus so hard on what we don't have that we forget to use what we do have.

For example, I think I have great hair. It's thick, but not too thick. It's straight, but it curls perfectly and stays. It has body, and it doesn't frizz in humidity. I have the hair gift, and I've always known it. And I've long been told I have the gift of humor. I love to make my friends laugh.

But for many years I failed to celebrate my gifts. I have this one friend—let's call her "Tammy." Wait . . . "Tammi," with an *i*. That fits better. More exotic. Anyway, whenever I was around Tammi, it

would take me 2.74 seconds to forget my hair and my humor and decide I was a boring, awkward sloth of a human. I was a slug; she was a butterfly. I was the "pity friend."

Tammi was jaw-droppingly pretty with perfect skin and a great figure. She somehow managed to have no cellulite after two kids (this is just freaky), and worst of all, she was as beautiful on the inside as she was on the outside. Just being in her space was defeating, not because of anything this poor woman would do, but because I was an emotional fruitcake focusing only on what I *wasn't* when I was next to her.

I loved Tammi and wanted to be around her, but I had to figure out how not to feel so bad about myself when we were together. At some point I made a brilliant decision: I would find *her* flaws and focus on those. A logical and sane approach, for sure, and excellent building blocks for any healthy friendship.

I told myself it might *look* like Tammi won the lottery in gifts, but she didn't. Tammi was terrible at math, she didn't like cats (okay, sure, she was highly allergic to them, but still), *and* she had a pinky toe-nail missing—like, no nail at all!

> **FOCUSING ON WHAT IS WRONG WITH PEOPLE, RATHER THAN WHAT IS LOVELY ABOUT THEM, RARELY WORKS.**

And I hate to say this publicly (even though I did change her name for her protection), but Tammi wore white shoes after Labor Day. Oh yes, she actually did such a thing. Obviously, there was much to pity about Tammi.

But despite the sophistication of my plan, I didn't feel any better. Turns out that focusing on what is wrong with people, rather than what is lovely about them, rarely works. In a healthy relationship you're supposed to fill each other's cups, be a blessing, and for the love of Pete, not focus on a girl's toe.

I've spent many painful years wondering why I didn't get the gifts other women had in abundance. I have always battled with my weight and have used it to measure whether I was worthy against other women. I have looked longingly at the beautiful, fabulous gifts of friends and strangers and asked myself, *Did God forget to give me gifts?* (Except for the hair gift, of course.)

I have finally stopped asking that question. It took some prodding and hinting and pushing, but when God started revealing more of my gifts over the last few years, I was at last ready to take notice.

FILL EACH OTHER'S CUP; BE A BLESSING.

Nine years ago, I entered the world of direct sales. Quite frankly, it wasn't anything I thought I would *ever* do. A younger me would have told you that tattooed pigs would fly before Dawn Barton would ever get into direct sales. But one day I jumped in to help my daughter, and then I grew to love the business myself.

The culture was unlike anything I had ever experienced. Women were building up other women. They were kind to each other and cheering for each other's successes. They were focusing on what every individual was good at, what her gifts were—and not focusing on the things she lacked. This was so different from the relationships I had experienced in every other work environment.

That culture of encouragement started to stir something in me. I kept hearing an internal voice: *You can be more. You have gifts you can share with the world.* It was a tiny giant inside me trying to rise.

YOU CAN BE MORE. YOU HAVE GIFTS YOU CAN SHARE WITH THE WORLD.

For the first few years, I kept pushing down the voice. I was not thin enough, poised enough, or skilled enough. So I continued to work at a mediocre level, putting in mediocre effort and getting mediocre results—with a recording of these self-induced, you're-not-good-enough lies playing over and over in my head.

But eventually this uplifting and positive culture began to work its way into my heart and my soul. That nurturing environment lovingly pushed me to stretch and get out of my comfort zone.

Slowly, month after month, I blossomed. Eventually, I became a multimillion-dollar producer and the number seven Mary Kay sales director in the nation.

So how did that happen? When did I shift my focus from the 698 gifts God didn't give me to the 784 He did?

Initially, during the company's training sessions for consultants, I believed I wasn't poised enough to succeed. I didn't stand just right or gesture like a beautiful hand model the way my friend Kali could. I was all over the place. I used my entire body to express myself. In fact, if you told me to sit on my hands and talk, there would be dead silence. It's the only way I can communicate with humans—my whole body and my entire face, all out.

Then one day I was attending a company event. The original speaker was sick and couldn't come, so somebody asked me to get up and talk. I was scared just thinking about all my flailing appendages. I knew it would be disastrous.

But it wasn't disastrous. I wasn't prepared, so it was me just being me—raw, real, and honest. And after it was over, a woman said to me, "Thank you for your authenticity and for being so genuine. For the first time I could see myself in you, and I believe I can do more."

I did not know her and I never saw her again, but the message stuck: be me. Quit trying to have someone else's gifts. God gave me Dawn's gifts. Embrace them. Use them. And be grateful for them!

I was almost forty years old when I learned I had the gift of speaking. I am one of those freakish people who can stand in front of thousands of people, talk, and truly *enjoy* it. I found this gift in the strangest of places—pushing to become a woman I never thought I could be through a business I swore I would never join.

So, yes, I have the gift of public speaking. I am authentic in my communication,

> **BE YOU. QUIT TRYING TO HAVE SOMEONE ELSE'S GIFTS. GOD GAVE YOU *YOUR* GIFTS. EMBRACE THEM. USE THEM. AND BE GRATEFUL FOR THEM!**

and it helps people relate to me. This statement took me years to learn and acknowledge about myself. Speaking is a gift, and I almost missed it because I was so preoccupied with every Tammi in my world.

Public speaking isn't all I can do. I can sew. (This is where you take a needle and thread with some fabric and transform it into wearable goods and curtains. I added that for you younger folk who

think clothing grows in the back room at Target.) Strategy and a competitive drive are also gifts of mine—though they may seem like curses to my opponents during game night, because, sister, I am there to crush and destroy.

I am surrounded by women who are blessed with incredible gifts. My dear friend Wendy has the gift of hospitality. A night at her house makes the Four Seasons look like a two-bit motel that charges by the hour. (I'm kidding, Four Seasons. I love you.) When I walk into the guest room at Wendy's place, there is a long basket on the bed filled with anything you could need, from toothbrushes to snacks. In the corner is my own personal Keurig, and she even switches out the photos in the room so that pictures of the two of us fill the frames. And though I have the personal coffee machine in the guest room, I never have to use it because the coffee is always hot downstairs and Wendy is waiting for me with a smile so big that any stress I was carrying when I showed up melts

> **FEW DECISIONS ARE MORE FREEING AND JOY-INDUCING THAN OPTING TO CELEBRATE ALL THE GIFTS—THE LITTLE ONES, THE BIG ONES, THE CRAZY ONES—IN MYSELF AND IN EVERYONE.**

away. (At my house she has to come into my bedroom and wake me to ask where the coffee is and if any mugs are clean.)

My mom can wiggle her ears, my friend Kali can clap louder than any human I've ever heard, and my husband instinctively waits until I am doing my most intense, focused writing to ask me an important question like, "Have you seen my measuring tape?"

Few decisions in my life have been more freeing and joy-inducing than opting to celebrate all these gifts in myself and the people I love—the little ones, the big ones, the crazy ones, and even the ones disguised as annoying things husbands do.

Why do we compare gifts we don't have to what someone else does have? It breaks us down. It makes us feel worse about ourselves. It's a little silly and a big waste of our energy.

We overlook our gifts because we believe they aren't as good as Tammi's gifts. Can you imagine if the great Andrea Bocelli stayed so fixated over his lack of eyesight that he chose not to sing? What if Julia Child was too sad to cook because she didn't have my flowing locks? (Granted, it is sad.) Can you imagine a world without those scrumptious cookbooks just because Julia didn't feel her

> **HOW MANY BEAUTIFUL, UNIQUE GIFTS FROM GOD ARE WE HIDING DUE TO OUR SELF-DOUBT?**

hair—or whatever physical feature—was good enough to be in the public eye? We all would have missed out on her talent.

I wonder how many beautiful, unique gifts God has given us that we are hiding due to our self-doubt. I bet there are gazillions around the world that have yet to see the light of day.

After I uncovered my gift and love for public speaking, I made a decision: *I will use, improve, and embrace what God has created in me.* When I arrive at the gates of heaven, I will not have God look me in the eyes and say, "Why didn't you use all of those glorious gifts I gave you?"

I refuse to let my first words to our Lord and Savior be: "Because I was worried that Tammi had better ones."

We may not get all the gifts, but the ones we have are ours, and they are 100 percent meant to be used. There's some real cause to celebrate. Look, together you and I have 1,482 scientifically unproven, magnificent gifts to share with others! Even if it takes you a while to discover them, and even if it's a messy process, God never wastes a mess—or a gift—as long as you share it.

MOM'S RED-HOT TOENAILS

Holding On to Joy for Dear Life

Blessed are you who weep
now, for you will laugh.

LUKE 6:21

IT WAS OCTOBER 14, the day before quarterly taxes were
due. My mother, the CPA, had been working tirelessly for weeks.
She came home from an exhausting day and plopped down to play
her card games on the computer while my father prepared dinner

for them a few feet away in the kitchen. They had been married forty-six years and adored one another.

They were chatting back and forth about the events of the day when my father suddenly heard a strange sound coming from the office. He walked into the room to find my mother's head down on the desk, her mouth open and making a slurping sound. He was sure she was having a stroke.

He grabbed the phone, dialed 911, and proceeded to perform CPR on my mother while waiting for the arrival of the ambulance. It pulled up within five minutes, and she was rushed to Saint Francis Hospital, less than a mile away. This quick action on my father's part, the fast arrival of the ambulance, and the hospital being so close were a perfect combination for my mother's survival.

We would later learn that an aneurysm had ruptured in my mother's brain. I found out about it from my sister Kim. She was crying when she called, but I could tell she was trying to be strong for whatever she was about to tell me.

"Dawn," she said, "something happened to Mom. They think she had a stroke, and they don't think she is going to make it through the night."

Why didn't I call her on Sunday? was the first thought that ran through my head. All the things I meant to do but didn't began flashing through my head. *This cannot be happening. God, please don't take my mom. Not my mom. I'm not ready. God, please save her.*

My mother was sixty-five years old, a beautiful, blue-eyed, red-headed Cajun woman, and she was brilliant. I mean, like, crazy, stupid smart—both of my parents were. We had the typical mother-daughter strains through my teens and twenties, but we had reached a beautiful place in our relationship, and I adored her. She understood me better than anyone in the world, even my own husband at times. I could not lose her, not now. I wasn't ready.

As I hung up the phone, my husband walked into the room and I fell into his arms, my knees collapsing, as I cried out for God to save my mother. I was helpless and devastated at the thought of losing her. I cried so hard and loud, as if the more intense my sobbing was, the more God would hear my cries.

About forty-five minutes later, the phone rang; it was Kim again. "Mom just responded to them," she said. "She squeezed their hands and mouthed her name. They said she has a fifty-fifty chance now." Kim was crying with joy, and I was elated at the possibility of my mom's survival. I had to get to her.

I was in Pensacola, Florida, and my mom was in Tulsa, Oklahoma. It was just after 9:00 P.M. on a Wednesday night. I couldn't get there until morning. The night was long, and I slept with my phone in my hand, praying it wouldn't ring. The next morning I boarded a plane, feeling a sense of panic about getting to her in time.

I needed to see her, to touch her, to hold her. I couldn't get there fast enough. I was in a perpetual state of pleading prayers with God. *Please don't take her. Please don't let her die.* It repeated in my head and slipped out of my mouth onto my lips as a whisper over and over. *Please don't let her die.*

Time has never moved slower than it did that day. Everything— the planes, the cars, the people—seemed to move in slow motion, no one caring that I was racing to my mother. I wanted to scream at the top of my lungs, "Move! Hurry! Don't you understand? She may be dying!"

I landed in Tulsa and my mom's sister—I call her Nanny—was arriving at the same time from Louisiana by car. I love my Nanny; she is my godmother and one of the most wonderful humans on the planet. She and my mom talk on the phone every single day as my Nanny makes her forty-five-minute drive home from work. I suspect they don't talk about much of anything, but they love it nonetheless. They are sisters, but more than that, they are best friends.

I ran outside of the airport terminal and saw her car coming around the corner. I opened the back door, threw in my suitcase, jumped into the front, and grabbed Nanny's hand tight. Tears were flowing down our faces; we understood the other's pain and how desperately we needed my mom to survive. We were five minutes into our drive to Saint Francis when my sister called to say Mom was being life-flighted to OU Medical Center in Oklahoma City. OU was a Level 1 neurotrauma center, and she needed that level of care to survive.

I had just landed in Tulsa and now she was being flown to Oklahoma City. I felt myself spiraling. The tears wouldn't stop. I felt like I was in one of those long hallways in a horror movie where the person is running and running and the hallway just keeps getting longer and longer. I couldn't get to my mom, and I've never felt so out of control and helpless in all my life. My tears and pleas to God continued all the way to Oklahoma City.

Oklahoma City is only an hour and half away by car, but as with all things that day, it felt like days. We ran by my parents' house to meet up with my dad and Kim and to grab a few things for my mom. Then, in three cars—Nanny and I in one, my dad in the second, and Kim in the third—we all burned rubber to Oklahoma City, a brigade of maniacs racing to a hospital. I was speeding and crying, believing if I got pulled over, I had a really good reason. (And truth be told, I thought if I did get pulled over, the cop might give me a police escort. It was a win-win either way in my completely unsound, utterly irrational mind.)

I rushed through the sliding glass doors of the neuro-ICU and straight to what appeared to be a military barricade: the nurses' desk. Just when I believed I was at the end of my horror scene, the hallway was stretching again. The commander of this military stronghold was a young, beautiful blonde with ringlet curls and a name tag that read "Ashley." I was out of breath and quickly explained who I was and that I needed to go back immediately.

Ashley paused for a moment. I could see that she didn't love what she was about to say, but she said it anyway: "I'm so sorry, but you cannot go back right now."

I just looked at her. I didn't think she understood. "I am the daughter who just flew in," I told her. "Then I drove a hundred miles. I have been racing to get to my mom for the entire day, and now she is only feet from me. I *have* to see her."

I tried not to sound mean, but I am pretty sure I sounded very, very mean.

Then her demeanor changed. I could see that I wasn't the first crazed family member who had come through the doors of that ICU. She knew how to handle lunatic, hurting loved ones.

"I'm very sorry, but she was just flown in, and we have to hook up all the monitors to her and get her situated in the bed and make sure she is stable. We can't do it with the room filled. But as soon as we are done, we will call you back. I promise."

Tears filled my eyes again. I hated this horrible woman with the most perfect, darling hair I'd ever seen. She was a monster disguised in curls.

We retreated to the waiting area, and time passed as slowly as it ever has. Finally, about an hour later, the doctor called us in. We walked down the hallway, passing each room with its big glass wall. Then we reached hers, 21C, on the right-hand side. We stepped inside.

My heart was not prepared for what my eyes were taking in. There she was, lifeless, her beautiful red hair covered in dried blood. Tubes out of her mouth and nose, cords and wires everywhere. I'd never seen anything like it. She didn't look like images shown on TV or in movies; Hollywood hadn't come close to visually capturing what a mother in ICU *really* looks like. It looked like they were keeping her alive through machines. Those first few moments wrecked me.

But after my mind digested what it was seeing, I was able to look past it all and see my mom—a beautiful, red-headed warrior. Her hand was in mine, my lips were kissing her cheek and forehead, and tears of

> **I WAS ABLE TO LOOK PAST IT ALL AND SEE MY MOM—A BEAUTIFUL, RED-HEADED WARRIOR.**

gratitude for God's grace were streaming down my cheeks. It was a miracle that we were here.

For the next seven days, the head nurse would come in and tell us that Mom might not survive. But I knew they were wrong. Marlene Goodson was one of the most headstrong, stubborn women I knew; she wasn't going to go down easily. The medical team was doing their job, but they didn't know the woman under those wires. *Just wait*, I thought. *She will show them.*

> IN DAYS FILLED WITH WINS AND DEFEATS, MAKE EVERY LITTLE WIN A JOY-FILLED CELEBRATION.

Our days were filled with wins and defeats. Every little win was a joy-filled celebration: fingers moving, toes wiggling, her hand lifting three inches off the bed. You name it, we made a huge deal about it.

But defeats happened daily. They came in different forms, like infections and fluid buildup, or looking into her beautiful blue eyes and seeing emptiness. She would look right back at me, but she wasn't there. My mom still wasn't awake.

Then, ten days in, it happened. We went through our same routine: squeezing hands, wiggling toes, and asking her to open her eyes. She slowly opened them, looked into my eyes, and, for the first time, I saw *her*. It was only for a few seconds, but she was there. I wish I knew how to describe what it's like to "see" a person in their eyes and know they are in there, and moments later to look in those same eyes and not see them at all. We take for granted how much the eyes truly are the windows to our souls.

As hard as our days could get, we still laughed a lot in that ICU room. You get a little wacky when you're cooped up in a hospital room all day and, well, we needed to entertain

> **AS HARD AS OUR DAYS COULD GET, WE STILL LAUGHED A LOT IN THAT ICU ROOM.**

ourselves. My mom's doctors mentioned she wouldn't remember anything from this time because of one of the drugs they were giving her, so my sister and I figured we had a green light to do something we'd always wanted to do: give Mom red toes!

My whole life I had never seen my mother put any color on her fingernails or her toenails unless it was the exact color of her skin or a clear coat. No, really—never. And, as you can imagine, she really disliked red in particular. She said redheads shouldn't wear red. Which is totally wrong. It just has to have the right undertones. We saw our opportunity and we took it—this was our chance to spice things up for our girl. Toes never looked so red or so fabulous as they did on my mother in that ICU. We gave her a little *va-va-voom*.

As she was recovering, joy was easy to find. We did whatever it took, much to the chagrin of the nurses, I'm sure. We sang to her. We danced to get her eyes to follow us (her eyes tracking with us was a huge win on any day). We prayed over her and sang worship songs out loud to her. Not once was I embarrassed or shy to sing (although, given my voice, I probably should have been) or to pray over her. We went all out, whatever it took.

And it worked.

Throughout those weeks, we became wonderful friends with our nurses—yes, even Ashley with the curls. She actually became one of my favorite nurses and cared for my mom beautifully, along with Bonnie, Heather, Mary Katherine, and many others. We came to love them all.

On our third week in the ICU, my mother turned a corner. She was responding, breathing on her own, and bit by bit, recovering every day. We moved Mom to a skilled nursing facility in Tulsa to be closer to Dad. She didn't walk out of the ICU—she was wheeled out, unable to even hold up her own head. But one hundred days later, she left that facility with a walker and her hand stretched in the air saying, "I'm out of here!" It will forever be one of my favorite moments.

NOT ONCE WAS I
EMBARRASSED OR SHY
TO SING OR TO PRAY
OVER HER. WE WENT ALL
OUT, WHATEVER IT TOOK.

Watching her recover day by day was like watching God work in real time for your eyes to see. It was a gift.

One month in an ICU and just over three months in the nursing home. Next stop: my house. She wasn't quite ready to go home, and we decided as a family my mom would come home with me to Florida.

BEING ABLE TO CARE FOR SOMEONE YOU LOVE AT SUCH AN INTIMATE LEVEL IS A GIFT.

Being able to care for someone you love at such an intimate level is a gift—a humbling, beautiful gift, filled with moments that can fuel your heart for a lifetime. I am so grateful that my father let me bring her to my home to work through the final phase of her recovery. It was a very special time for all of us—Craig, Ella, me, and Mom—although she doesn't remember much of it.

I'm not going to lie—we did have a lot of laughs, maybe at her expense on occasion. The aneurysm affected my mom's short-term memory, and as her brain was healing, it did some really funny things.

Her short-term memory was affected a little, but her long-term memory was great. She liked to play the "aneurysm card" every now and again—but if you let her sucker you into a trivia game, she'll crush you every single time because she is still crazy smart.

During the week when the therapists would come to work with her, they would give her verbal quizzes to test her memory. I failed every single time, and I have not had a brain aneurysm. So, the way I see it, she is fully healed and the rest of us just have really bad memories.

These days my mother is home with my dad, doing "a whole lotta nothin'." They are joyfully retired, relaxing and loving this season of their lives. For years we hoped they would move, but they just didn't feel like packing.

That is, until I lovingly asked them to please move closer to us, which looked a little more like relentless begging, pushing, and prodding. They are now next door to us in Florida, happier than they ever thought possible being so close to their most precious child. I may have added that extra part at the end, but I'm pretty sure this is how they feel.

Laughter and smiles are a constant in their home. I never dreamed that the side effect of a brain aneurysm could be joy, but it literally has been. Before her brain aneurysm, my mom was a CPA, running her company and working a great deal, and her stress was high. My father was retired, and they saw each other in the evenings and during the occasional lunch.

Today, my mother has a childlike joy about her, which I believe to be a gift of the aneurysm. She is one of the happiest people I know. She sings, she laughs, she's funny and enjoys life, and for this I am so grateful. I never could have imagined that so much joy could have come from a nearly fatal ruptured brain aneurysm. But it did because, well, that's God. Next to Him, my mom may now be the single best joy creator I know. And she taught us well. Even if we have to look high and low, down in the cracks or in the corners of a hospital room, we know it's there to be found—or created from thin air. Wherever we are, all we need is that willingness to find it.

And maybe a bottle of red-hot toenail polish.

11

MY LOBSTER

Learning to Fight for Each Other

Above all, love each other deeply, because
love covers over a multitude of sins.

1 PETER 4:8

WHEN I DID AN outline for this book, this chapter was not
included. Although it represents a very big piece of my life, it is not
my story to tell; it is my husband's. But as I was nearing the end of
the book, I felt God prompting me to tell this story, so I spoke with
Craig about it. It is with his loving, brave permission that I share it
with you.

I met Craig Barton on Match.com when I first moved to Florida. He used a ten-year-old photo of himself in his flight suit (which is about the sexiest thing any man can wear, in my opinion), smiling sweetly and relaxing on a sofa. I used a photo in which my body and face were angled just right to give the illusion that I was thin and fit.

I guess you could say our relationship was born out of lies, but it worked. We talked and emailed for a couple of weeks, and I felt as if I had known him all my life. I think I loved him before I ever met him in person. We arranged for our first meeting to be at the Starbucks in Barnes & Noble in Destin, Florida. If all went well, we would go to dinner.

It was November 29, 2003. I was nervous and spent hours getting dressed, curling my hair, and applying my makeup just right—not so heavy that I'd be mistaken for Tammy Faye and not so light that he'd think I was a natural girl who liked to hike or camp. I wore my blackest black outfit in an attempt to look as thin as humanly possible, and I topped it off with a long black coat. He was sure to think I was a tiny, delicate flower, dipped in black.

I arrived at Barnes & Noble thirty minutes early and looked for a book to buy him. I found the perfect one: *The Worst-Case Scenario Little Book for Dating*. It included how-tos like "How to Escape from a Bad Date" and "How to Save Your Date from Choking." I thought it was a riot. When he walked in, he was handsome and taller than I'd expected (he's six feet, two inches). He had kind eyes and a warm smile. I gave him the book, he laughed, and we skipped the coffee and went on to dinner.

(Many years later, a friend asked him what he thought of me when he first saw me, and he responded with one word: "*perfect*." Every time I think of that, I smile from ear to ear.)

We dined at an upscale restaurant, and Craig talked nonstop for three hours. He talked and talked and talked. I barely said five words. Now, if you know us, this is funny because I am the talker and he is the introvert, a man of few words. But he was nervous and had been drinking before we met up, so he was very relaxed. I had no idea that this behavior would nearly be the downfall of our marriage.

One week after that first date, I knew I would marry the wonderful Craig Barton—and four months later, I did. I'd never been with a man who loved me so completely, and I loved the way he loved my daughter Makenzie too. He was and is the kindest, sweetest man we've ever known.

Craig is originally from California, raised by his lovely mother, Rosalie. Yes, I truly do like my mother-in-law. She was on her own after Craig's father left when Craig was five. She is hardworking, loving, and a fiercely independent woman.

From the age of ten, Craig knew he wanted to be a pilot. He

knew the path he wanted to take and focused hard on it. This meant enlisting in the reserves in college and then joining the marines to become a Cobra helicopter pilot. Later, he became an instructor pilot and continued in that role in the naval reserves, and he eventually became a commercial airline pilot.

Now, you may not be very familiar with the military pilot world, so let me just tell you: there used to be a lot of drinking in it. For Craig, an introverted man, it was a way to have fun—but also a way to feel more comfortable around other people. Craig and his fellow pilots worked hard and played harder. Craig embraced beer as his good friend; it became a part of who he was and how he coped for the next twenty years.

I don't know what other people's lives look like when they are struggling with addiction in the home, but I can tell you about ours. During the early years of our marriage, it was the same pattern over and over: he would start to drink more regularly, his drinking would increase in frequency, we would have a huge blow-up fight about it, and then he would back off the drinking for a while. This cycle continued for years. Sometimes the length between cycles was longer, but the results were always the same.

I hated Craig when he drank. It was as if there were two different men in my home: the Craig I loved, and this horrible, mean jerk I despised. He was unkind and hateful. He was never physically violent toward me or anyone else, but his words were like weapons and chipped away at me over and over, year after year.

Now, let's be clear: I was not some perfect, adoring wife who sat innocently in a corner. I was hard to be married to. I spent too much money, I was controlling, and I wasn't always easy to communicate with. I suspect now, looking back, that some of my flaws fed some of Craig's attempts to escape through alcohol. But for now, let's just blame Craig for all of it. Okay, I'm kidding . . . but I'm not.

ONLY THE PERSON DRINKING IS RESPONSIBLE FOR THAT PERSON'S DRINKING.

In case anyone reading this feels they are the cause of someone else's drinking, I want you to know something: *only the person drinking is responsible for that person's drinking.* You did *not* cause it. You *cannot* cure it. You *cannot* control it. Those are some very wise words from my Al-Anon meeting. I don't care if your loved one blames you daily. You are *not* at fault, no matter what they tell you.

In October 2010, Craig was in the navy reserves and flying for a commercial airline. Many of our friends were being deployed, so Craig opted to proactively sign up for a military tour. It was a one-year stint at Isa Air Base in the Middle East—Bahrain, to be exact. He was to be the XO, also known as the second-in-command.

To be honest, if you're going to be deployed to the Middle East, this is *not* a bad gig. It's fairly safe, with plenty of access to the conveniences of the Western world, and we had many options for communicating daily. But that's little comfort when you're saying a tearful goodbye in the Pensacola airport three weeks after your husband signs up for an active military tour.

In Bahrain, Craig worked in huge tents that were converted into makeshift offices, and he lived in a small trailer far from the bathrooms. He had great stories to tell, like when he spent Thanksgiving with the American ambassador at the American consulate and when he met Robin Williams and other celebrities who came on military tours. I didn't feel too sorry for him.

Six months into his deployment, he came back to the States for his allotted two-week visit. During this visit, I found the lump on my right breast, but it wasn't for another six weeks, long after Craig was back in Bahrain, that we would discover it was Stage 3 cancer. That's when we decided together he would complete his deployment, and my family and friends would help me through my chemo treatments until he finished four months later. He returned home at the height of my sickness when I was at my worst.

CANCER CAN BE HARDER ON THE FAMILY THAN ON THE PATIENT.

Sometimes I think cancer can be harder on the family than on the patient. Craig was taking care of Ella, the house, and me. He was incredible, selfless, and epitomized the meaning of our marital vow "in sickness and in health." You don't grasp the true significance of that vow until you are lying in bed and losing control of your bodily functions because you are so sick from chemotherapy poisoning. When you wake from sleep with diarrhea all over yourself, your bed, and your carpet, there is little dignity left in you. But never, not once, did Craig flinch. He would clean me, carry me to the bathroom, clean me again, clean the beds and floors, and lovingly kiss me as if nothing had happened. *This* is what "in sickness and in health" means. I don't know if I could have been as good if the roles were reversed.

During Craig's deployment and all through my cancer, the drinking was minimal. But after years of cancer, the demon of alcohol began to rear its ugly head again. The cycle was the same: Craig would be out for four days on a work trip, then home and sober for one day, then he'd get drunk, be a mean jerk, feel bad the next day, and then leave on a trip again. I looked forward to him being gone and hated when that drunken Craig was around. I missed the kind, loving Craig desperately.

I prayed every single day for God to heal him, for God to take this horrible disease out of him and our lives. I prayed for years and heard nothing.

Then, one April, everything blew up. Craig's mom was about to move from California to be near us in Florida, and Craig was remodeling her new home before she arrived. During this time he was taking vacation from work and spending days on end preparing her house.

Although he was making progress on the house, Craig's drinking was at an all-time high. My mother-in-law's new home was ten houses down from ours, and one afternoon I walked over there to peek in. I found Craig so drunk he couldn't speak or walk. As I looked through the house, I realized he had graduated from beer and was hiding vodka bottles here.

The next two days were the same, and I told him not to come home. Craig stayed over at his mom's empty house for a few days, and then, one afternoon in a drunken haze, he called a good friend and said that he needed help with his drinking. The friend contacted me, and I immediately began to look into next steps.

The morning after Craig made the phone call to his friend, he was sober and furious to learn I had started the process for him to get counseling. He told me in his fury that he did not need help, that I was ruining his life. He hated me, and I hated myself. I questioned everything that was going on and regretted that I had called a therapist.

Eventually, though, Craig gave in and started counseling. At first he continued to blame me and didn't speak to me for days, but at least he was getting help.

Then, finally, he began to soften. I could hear the old Craig again. He let me join some of his counseling sessions. It was eye-opening, learning about this awful disease of alcoholism. I learned what happens in the brain and the body, and I began to understand how little control Craig had over it. I heard the stories of other people suffering from alcoholism and realized that God stopped this for Craig in its early stages. Compared with the destruction and pain addiction caused in others' lives, I knew we were lucky.

Craig's decision to stop drinking was just the beginning of our healing. Craig took a year off work to focus on strengthening his newly sober self. We had to learn to communicate better. We went through therapy. It wasn't easy, but I was elated to have Craig back.

I can honestly say there was a point where I didn't believe God could repair what was destroyed during those years. The emotional hurt and the pain were just so deep. But He did heal us, and through that process our faith grew—and so did our love for each other.

It's hard to see the big picture when you are in the thick of years

like these, but now I look back at that season of our lives and realize God was there with us the whole time, working for our good.

As that season of our married life came to a blessed close, a new one started. And it wasn't easy, certainly not when combined with my mother's brain aneurysm and her month-long stay in neuro-ICU before moving to a skilled nursing facility in Tulsa, Oklahoma. Because this happened when Craig wasn't working, I had the flexibility to be with my mother through that frightening time. And best of all, when she was released, I was able to bring her home to live with us for three months until she was well enough to go back home to my dad.

THERE IS LOVE WHERE I BELIEVED NONE COULD LIVE.

If Craig hadn't decided to address his drinking problem, if he hadn't been home for a year, I would not have had the gift of caring for my mother—which was one of the greatest gifts of my life.

Today, there is joy in our marriage and in our lives. There is love where I believed none could live, and there is beauty in knowing we will grow old together, because together we went into the valley and together we climbed out of it.

I have a friend who's been married a very long time, and one time I asked her the secret to her successful marriage. "Well," she said, "we never fell out of love at the same time. One partner was always fighting for the other."

Craig Barton fought for me through cancer, and I fought for him through addiction. And by the grace of God, we made it through.

It may seem like we're all on a collision course with these life-changing struggles, with each other, and with events in our lives that are beyond our control. But since we share life with each other, us humans, we get an up-close-and-personal view of human brokenness. Still, we need each other.

> **TOGETHER WE WENT INTO THE VALLEY AND TOGETHER WE CLIMBED OUT OF IT.**

And I'm confident that love will bring us through hopelessness. Grace will bring us through. Sheer grit will bring us through. When it comes to the ones we love, let's never give up the fight for each other.

KIM'S RAK

Discovering the Power of Random Acts of Kindness

Faith in action is love, and love in action is
service. By transforming that faith into living
acts of love, we put ourselves in contact
with God Himself, with Jesus our Lord.

MOTHER TERESA

ON OCTOBER 3, 2016, her text came in: "Please call me."

I was already feeling stretched as I juggled the continuous texts, emails, and calls of a crazy workday, and at that moment I was walking into an appointment.

"I can't right now," I quickly responded. "I'm in a meeting. Can I call you later?"

There was a long pause, followed by: "I have breast cancer." Everything stopped. Work was instantly insignificant.

My baby sister, Kim, had breast cancer. How was that even possible? We had no family history of any cancer, and now both of us had been hit in a five-year span. It seemed beyond unfair.

Kim and I were almost four years apart and as different as two people could be. We were day and night. She was low-maintenance and hippy-esque while I was squarish and more conservative. I was boring; she was fun. (In my defense, I wasn't exactly *boring*. I just didn't do well after 9:00 P.M. But you should see me from about 6:00 A.M. to 3:00 P.M. I'm a blast.)

We had our differences since birth, and for most of our lives, we argued about everything under the sun. Eventually we'd agree to disagree and accept that we were just different. But of course, I loved her; she was my sister. She was smart, beautiful, and funny, and she gave the best bear hugs in the world. When she loved you, she loved all out. Totally and completely.

This cancer, this beast, was attacking my baby sister, and I was furious. Shouldn't there be a limit on how many people in one family can have a particular ailment? Shouldn't the pain of the world be more evenly divided? *Here's your pain, here's your pain, here's your pain—oh, wait, you've had yours already. No worries, you're clear.* This seems like a much better way of making the world go 'round. There should definitely be term limits on pain.

As the news soaked in, my stomach tightened and a million little moments of my own cancer journey flashed through my mind. The hair loss, the exhaustion, the sickness, the swelling from steroids, the constant battle each day. The protective older sister in me was so mad that my

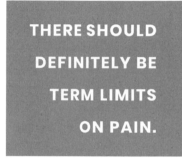

THERE SHOULD DEFINITELY BE TERM LIMITS ON PAIN.

baby sister would have to go through it all alone. Just Kim and the dogs at home, and her son, Daniel, far off in another state. I knew this was going to be hard and it wasn't fair.

I wanted to hug her and never let go and promise that it was all going to be okay, but we were basically a million miles apart—she was in Tulsa and I was in Pensacola, a distance that makes hugging hard. I hated the distance, but I knew she could make it through. I had survived Stage 3 cancer five years before, and she was diagnosed with Stage 2. She had a long road ahead of her, but she was going to be okay.

For so many years, Kim and I had not been as close as two sisters should be, but cancer seemed to wipe it all away in seconds. I was in full Protective Big Sister mode from there on out.

That insidious cancer brought us closer. We spoke almost daily and talked more in that season than we probably had in our entire lives. I understood where she was, and I was grateful I had the experience and perspective to help with her battle.

In true Kim fashion, she began her cancer journey like a champ and found joy and humor at every turn she could. She made jokes about it on Facebook and answered every "How are you doing?" with some funny little self-effacing comment. She was the reassuring one, making those around her laugh and smile.

But as the weeks moved on, I could see that the effects of the chemo were intensifying. We were talking only once or twice a week as she waged war on cancer and battled through rest and sleep. She was exhausted, emotionally and physically, and having a hard time with the side effects of chemo. I wouldn't hear from her for almost a week until the effects would wear off for a few days.

Then, on a Friday afternoon, she called. Her voice was upbeat with traces of joy once again. I could hear the smile on her face through the phone.

"Hey, guess what? I just got a card from Paula!" she exclaimed. Paula was my next-door neighbor. She'd met Kim many times, and we'd spoken several times about my sister's battle. "It was my first card."

Wait, did she just say "first card"? First card today, or this week maybe?

No. It was quite literally the first card anyone had sent her since her cancer journey had begun. I felt like I had been gut-punched. How could this possibly be? Why wasn't she showered with love during this horrible time?

I was blessed with cards every single day during my cancer journey. My friends, coworkers, and church were incredible, and I naively assumed that Kim's experience would be the same. I believed that when you got diagnosed with cancer, people always sent cards and flowers, set up meal trains, and popped over to help where they could. I was wrong. Kim did not have the same kind of support system.

It never once occurred to me to ask about these things. I felt like the most thoughtless person on the planet. What kind of woman, much less sister, doesn't even ask about this? I had to do something; I wanted to make it right. At this point, sending her a card seemed flippant and meaningless. I needed to take action.

Step One: "Unfriend" Kim on Facebook so she couldn't see what I was doing.

Step Two: Tell the world our stories on a Facebook Live video.

Step Three: Pray for God to move.

I thought about it for approximately two hours before going

live on Facebook. I was emotional and frustrated. I desperately wanted—no, *needed*—people to care, mostly because of my overwhelming love for Kim, but I think there was a piece of me that felt guilty. Guilty that I had received so much love and support through my cancer journey and she had little to none through hers. And I felt guilty that I had never even thought to ask about it all—I just made stupid assumptions.

I went live with my video and prayed that someone was listening. I told Kim's story and said how she was navigating cancer treatments while living alone. I shared about the card from Paula and explained how different my journey through cancer had been. I asked if anyone watching could take two minutes to send a quick message of encouragement, love, and prayer to her. I even gave out her email and mailing address. (In hindsight this may not have been the smartest move, but God was on it. No data mining.) It was a quick three-minute video on a Friday afternoon.

Four days later I got a call from Kim. "What did you do?"

She was in tears, and I could barely understand her words. "The mailman came to my door with forty-seven cards and two packages," she managed to get out. "And I have a ton of emails. I can't believe you did this!"

She was laughing and crying simultaneously as she read cards and notes to me. I loved hearing her happiness through the phone.

It was music to my ears despite all she was going through; she was genuinely joyful.

The showering of love continued, with twenty to thirty cards getting stuffed into her mailbox each day. This was more than I ever could have hoped or prayed for. I was in awe of the kindness of people, most of them strangers to Kim.

Simple random acts of kindness were dramatically and beautifully changing her days. It showed me we can make a huge difference doing something we think is so small. Those small things became an enormous gift to Kim.

After receiving these little kindnesses, Kim and I were talking more often and our conversations were fun. Christmas came, and it was only a few more days until I would finally see her at our family's annual New Year's Eve gathering. I couldn't wait to hug her.

> **SIMPLE RANDOM ACTS OF KINDNESS CAN DRAMATICALLY AND BEAUTIFULLY CHANGE OUR DAYS.**

Every year our entire family on my mother's side rents cabins on the water at Chicot State Park in Louisiana. We gather for a few days of visiting, laughing, and consuming insane amounts of fantastic and unhealthy food (mostly Cajun food, our favorite!). It's a cherished time together every year, and we love every minute of it.

Kim arrived at Chicot before me. I walked into the cabin, and there she was—bald, pale, and smiling from ear to ear. I thought she looked great. She wrapped her arms around me and pulled me into that famous Kim bear hug. Kim was known for her hugs. Her hug was the safest, most comfy place in the world. Oh, how I had missed those hugs. I loved us being in each other's arms.

All of us spent the weekend talking and laughing in between her naps and rests. There was a new, different connection between us as sisters, a connection forged by the pain of cancer, and it brought out a deep love for each other; I just hated that it took us so long to find it. I wished it hadn't taken this dramatic circumstance to remind us what was important, but I was also grateful for it.

A CONNECTION FORGED BY THE PAIN OF CANCER BROUGHT OUT A DEEP LOVE FOR EACH OTHER.

We had a wonderful few days and even stopped eating for a few hours to take family photos. It had been almost ten years since the last family photo session, and it was time. The men complained, the women dressed up and tried to keep the kids clean, and we pulled it off. The Cajun photo shoot was a success!

The time passed too quickly, and the day of our departure was upon us. It was time to say goodbye—back to Tulsa for Kim and Pensacola for me. We stood outside my car, and I was once again wrapped in her bear hug, never wanting to let go.

When Kim pulled away, she grabbed my shoulders and looked me in the eyes, hers filled with tears. "Thank you for what you did," she said. "You changed my life. Those cards changed my life."

The tears fell down her face and then mine. We hugged as long as we could, holding each other and crying and treasuring each other. Then we pulled apart one last time, looking at each other in one of the most pure, loving ways we ever had.

My face wet with tears, I climbed into our car and began driving away, waving and blowing kisses to her out the window. Then we turned the corner and she was gone.

As I drove, I thought about what Kim had said and how passionately she thanked me. Who could have imagined that a bunch of cards and emails could change a woman's life so completely in such a short amount of time? That in those cards, Kim would feel God's loving arms around her and find peace, and even joy, in her journey? I was reminded that God is a God of details and He knew. He knew the dramatic turn our lives were about to take.

God gave us the gift of a deep and loving sisterly bond that was closer and more beautiful than ever before. He did away with the memories of arguments and a sometimes-strained relationship and put in its place a perfect, unconditional love.

God moved in the hearts and minds of hundreds of people—friends and strangers alike—to show Kim the abundance of His love, and He gave Kim the gift of experiencing this outpouring of love through the lonely, difficult days of her sickness.

GOD IS A GOD OF DETAILS.

But most of all, God gave us the gift of a family gathering, complete with photos—no one missing, no one sick, just all of us together as a family in laughter and love.

We didn't understand until weeks later that this seemingly normal family gathering was, in fact, the most precious gift of all: the gift of happy memories. What we believed was a simple family reunion was a beautiful and precious farewell to my wonderful Kim.

A mere eight days later, on January 10, my sweet sister unexpectedly passed away in her sleep. I still don't have the words to articulate the brokenness of my heart. My words about Kim have been the most difficult to write because the pain is the freshest.

Honestly, I am still in awe that God gave us the gift of saying goodbye, even though we didn't know that's what it was at the time. My family is forever grateful for God's gift of love, healing, and the

precious time we had with Kim in the last months of her life. I'm able to smile because I know she is currently giving bear hugs in heaven.

Prior to this, I'm embarrassed to say I never thought much about the impact of a random act of kindness (or a RAK, as I call it now)—doing them or receiving them. I haven't been good at randomly seeing others' needs and acting on them. I would love to say something like, "I'm just not wired that way," or "It's just not my gift." But the reality is, I just didn't care enough to get out of my own selfish head. I didn't think it mattered, and quite frankly, I can't ever find a stamp around this house.

Sometimes it takes great big things to make the little things so obvious. Sometimes it takes seeing a person's life become so beautifully changed by a trickling of small, random acts of kindness—even from strangers—to realize you can't sit back and ignore the impact it has. Ignorance and inconvenience are no longer valid excuses.

YOU HOLD THE POWER TO CHANGE THE WORLD, BECAUSE IT IS IN THE ACCUMULATION OF THE SMALL THAT THE EXTRAORDINARY HAPPENS.

Each of us holds the key to changing the world; we each have the ability to do small, random acts of kindness for others. Be it a card, a gift, an action, or a word, you hold the power to change the world.

I am ready to be a part of the extraordinary. Stamps or no stamps, I'm ready.

#KIMSMILLION

Finding Healing in a Legacy

Jesus said to her, "I am the resurrection and the
life. The one who believes in me will live, even
though they die; and whoever lives by believing
in me will never die. Do you believe this?"

JOHN 11:25-26

I HAD DECIDED: 2016 was going to be a record-breaking
year for my team. We would skyrocket from $383,000 in annual
sales to more than $1 million in just twelve months. In the fifty-five-
year history of our direct sales company, few had ever produced a

million in annual sales, and no one in our company had ever jumped from where we were to a million—until now. We were going to be that history-making team. I knew it.

Our fiscal year ran from July 1 to June 30, and when July 1 hit, we were race horses bursting free from our starting gates. We were ready to set records, and we would do it with a smaller team than any team that had ever tried. It was exhilarating, and we were perfectly poised for this twelve-month, million-dollar race.

Three months after the start of our monumental year, Kim was diagnosed with breast cancer. She was now in her own race—against cancer—but she was still excited for us to achieve our goal. She asked if she could come on stage with me at Seminar, our year-end company event. I told her yes, of course, and then she said she would need to borrow a dress. I remember her adding, "Well, at least I'll be skinny for it." She was always making light of her diagnosis.

She was one of my biggest cheerleaders, and I loved her for it.

At the end of December, Craig, Ella, and I headed to Chicot in Louisiana for the precious family reunion where we took pictures we'd end up treasuring the rest of our lives. But at that point my team was six months into our sales race, and for the first time, I was starting to toy with the idea that we may not achieve our million-dollar goal. The numbers were too far off, and our team was just too small. I wasn't sure how to pull out of it, what to do, or how to handle it, so I decided to strategize about how to tell my team we would not make this lofty goal once I returned home.

New Year's Day came and went, and I formulated a message in my head: "We're having an incredible year, but it's just not enough. I can't see how we could do it." Soon I would tell my team.

But when my sister died unexpectedly on Tuesday, January 10, I was shocked and devastated. I never imagined I would lose her. I know that sounds naive, given her diagnosis of breast cancer and all the treatments she'd had. But it was unconscionable to me that she would not survive this.

Kim passed on a Tuesday, and I flew to Tulsa to be with my parents on the following Wednesday. For the first time in my life, I felt our roles reverse; I was the one caring for them as they waded through their unimaginable grief.

My mother was in shock and had simply fallen apart.

My father was working so hard to be the stoic man he'd always been. He was our backbone, and until this, I could count on one hand the times I had seen my father cry. But I've never heard him weep as much as he did that Friday afternoon as we laid her to rest. It broke my heart to see and hear his cries. They are etched in my mind for a lifetime.

Saying goodbye to my parents after laying my sister to rest

was heart-wrenching. I boarded my flight that Saturday, sat in my seat, and let the tears flow. I kept my head turned toward the window, looking at the tarmac, to hide my wet face from those around me. My baby sister was gone, and I didn't care about work or goals. I knew I would not hit my million-dollar goal, and that was fine. Honestly, there was a relief of sorts. I had just lost my sister, and no one would blame me for pulling back and not working to finish this grandiose goal. My sister was gone. I was allowed to fall apart.

And then I heard her. I heard Kim in my mind, saying, *Don't blame me for not hitting your goal!* It made me chuckle. But this was not the time to think about work or goals, and I didn't give the moment much more thought.

> **DON'T BLAME ME FOR NOT HITTING YOUR GOAL!**

I returned home, and my sole objective was to climb into bed. I wanted to stay there the rest of my life, curled up, covers over my head, hiding from this new reality. I wanted to fall into a sea of sadness and mourning, and wrap myself in grief. I wanted the world to go away.

The next day was supposed to be the start of my company's big leadership conference in New Orleans. I had registered and paid to attend months earlier, but I knew I wouldn't go, not now.

My heart was too broken, and I just wanted to be in bed for weeks, maybe months.

Within hours of returning home from Tulsa, my bed plans were diverted when I received a message from a dear work friend who suggested I should still attend the conference. "So many of your dearest friends will be there to shower you with love," she said. "It would be good to be busy."

I was shocked and I was angry. How could she even suggest such a thing? I had just lost my sister. I was furious and in awe of her insensitivity. Phones went off. I was going to bed.

My bed felt like heaven, a hideaway from the world. My room is white—white sheets, white linen curtains, white walls. It's bright and most days it gives a glorious feeling of peace, but not now. It felt stark and lonely. I made it as dark as I could. I cried, I slept, I ate. And then I cried and slept some more.

Following several hours of this, I heard Kim's voice again. *So you have the chance to go to New Orleans, but you're going to stay in bed and cry over me? You big dummyhead.*

Dummyhead was Kim's word, and it made me laugh every time she said it. Kim *loved* New Orleans, maybe more than any human in the history of the world. She adored all things Louisiana, and she was always up for a good time. If you're ever in New Orleans enjoying a night out, raise your glass and give a toast to the most wonderful baby sister in the world. She loved the food, the drinks, the people—everything. Staying away from New Orleans *because* of Kim would have been, well, something only a dummyhead would do.

I don't know what on earth possessed me, but I got up, went to the living room, and told Craig I was going to the conference. Then I called my parents, and they agreed I should go. So I went.

It was one of the best decisions I have ever made. I can't tell you about anything I learned, or any events I attended, or anywhere we went; all I can tell you is how I felt. I felt loved. I felt as if hundreds of women wrapped me in their arms and carried me through those few days.

> THAT LOVE WAS THE CATALYST FOR A DRAMATIC SHIFT IN MY THINKING.

That love was the catalyst for a dramatic shift in my thinking. Ten days before, I was certain we could not achieve the million-dollar goal. And now I knew I *had* to achieve this goal. If I achieved this goal, I'd have the opportunity to stand on a stage in front of ten thousand women in Dallas and tell the world about my sister Kim. The thought of that one moment in time became my driving force to finish.

I wouldn't miss this goal because Kim died. I'd finish this goal because Kim lived.

My parents were thrilled with my decision, and Craig was completely behind me. We all understood this wasn't about selling products—it was about sharing Kim's legacy. I told my team we'd dedicate the rest of our fiscal year to honor Kim, and everything we did for the next six months became "Kim's Million." #KimsMillion was plastered everywhere—our social media posts, our shirts, our cups, our tote bags, and anywhere else we could share the story.

> **I WOULDN'T MISS THIS GOAL BECAUSE KIM DIED. I'D FINISH THIS GOAL BECAUSE KIM LIVED.**

Appointment after appointment, I shared about Kim and what we were doing in her honor. I became obsessed. I still grieved and cried through those months, and I have no doubt working so hard was an escape from dealing with her loss, but I also felt God's blessing on what was unfolding. I knew we were called to do this. He was in everything we did, and even when it was hard and I couldn't see how it would come together, I still felt Him saying, "Trust Me."

Hearing "trust Me" and *doing* it are two very different things. I didn't feel like God was saying, "Trust Me, girl. This is done. Sit down, relax, and kick back. It's all good." God can move mountains, but don't be surprised when He throws you a shovel. I knew the

SATURDAY, JUNE 29, 2019

To do

SUNDAY, JUNE 30, 2019

Today

6 am
7 am
8 am
9 am
10 am
11 am
12 pm
1 pm
2 pm
3 pm
4 pm
5 pm
6 pm
7 pm
8 pm
9 pm

To do

All Out, All Day!

↓

Notes

Last day of the
MK Year!
#Kimsmillion

GOD CAN MOVE MOUNTAINS, BUT DON'T BE SURPRISED WHEN HE THROWS YOU A SHOVEL.

shovel was in my hands, and it was up to me to dig and dig and dig. And when I did, the blessings came: I was invigorated by connecting with friends and strangers, and I was touched by the passion and energy in my team.

But even through all the blessings, I couldn't see a way to hit our goal. I am a strategist. I love a good spreadsheet and numbers. I can take a situation and tell you how to get to a finish line, and I can also tell you if things are just not going to happen because numbers don't lie. My team and I were too far away, and when I looked at everything on paper, I could see, big faith or not, our goal was not going to come together.

It was the middle of May, we were forty-five days away from the finish line, and those numbers were screaming, "Girl, pack that bag and buy a ticket to some place with tiny umbrellas in your drinks because there is no way you are going to pull off the million-dollar miracle."

So I did what any self-respecting, soon-to-be-monumental failure would do: I called my best friend to cry. I told Kali I needed to come over right away, and that's what I did. I ran up the stairs to her bedroom, and we both sat on the bed, cross-legged, facing each other. I looked at Kali with tears in my eyes, and I told her we weren't going to make it. I had crunched the numbers a million different ways, and it was just not there. No matter what scenario I had run, I could not see us finishing our million-dollar goal.

She took my hands into hers, tears filled *her* eyes, and she smiled and said, "I'm so glad."

Now, just to be clear, this is *not* the response you want to hear from your best friend when you are explaining that you are about to fail bigger than the rebooted *Dallas*. Then she said, "Because now you've crossed from strategy to faith, and this is where God gets all the glory."

That statement right there— *where God gets all the glory*—I recognized immediately as the truth. If this goal was going to honor God and my sister, then it had to be a race finished in the faith zone. And it was.

> YOU'VE CROSSED FROM STRATEGY TO FAITH, AND THIS IS WHERE GOD GETS ALL THE GLORY.

In the last five minutes, on the very last day, it was done. We achieved our million-dollar goal because of a million little miracles, every single day for twelve months. An unlikely group of women were brought together for a year such as this, and they did something miraculous.

Romans 8:28 says, "We know that in all things God works for the good of those who love him, who have been called according to his purpose."

I cannot tell you how often I have struggled with that verse. How can there be good that comes out of a child's death? Or out of the loss of my sister? It seems impossible. But there was joy and there was good that came because we lost Kim. Was it good that she died? Absolutely not. I hate it, and I'm still angry and hurt, but there were blessings and grace amid the pain.

A small group of women broke records because of her. We grew exponentially in our faith and believed in ourselves more than we ever imagined. We had a front-row seat to watch God work in miraculous ways, and I know without a doubt we would not have done these things had we not lost Kim.

Six months and two weeks after I lost my sister, I stood in the middle of a stage in Dallas and shared the story of my baby sister with ten thousand women. My mother stood on the floor front and center, tears streaming down her face, filming me with camera in hand. A friend of mine took a photo of her in that moment. It is and always will be one of my favorite photos. Not because it was my mom watching *me*, but because it was us, in a moment, sharing Kim with the world. World, meet Kim. It was perfect.

Kim's legacy will live on and good will come from the heartache of her loss. There's a ripple effect of good in her story—a beautiful example of God's love passing on and on and on, even in pain.

Loss can immobilize us, blindside us, and take us down deep into a valley where it seems the tears will never end. But when we lose someone precious, maybe through our tears, we'll see a light to lead us forward. Or hear a voice to push us on. To share the gifts they gave us and the joy they brought us, to expand on the love they've planted in this world—until it grows a millionfold.

IT'S A ONE-WOMAN JOB

Finding the Courage to Choose

May the God of hope fill you with all joy and peace
as you trust in him, so that you may overflow
with hope by the power of the Holy Spirit.

ROMANS 15:13

LET'S BEGIN THIS CHAPTER by acknowledging I am probably going to hurt someone's feelings with what I am about to say. For that, I'm sorry. I wish I could wrap my arms around you and whisper, "I get it, I understand, and I love you," because I do. But sometimes it takes a good girlfriend to say the hard things, so . . .

Oh, hold on. Do you need to go grab a glass of wine first? I can wait. Okay. Here it is: you finding joy is *your* choice. It's *your* decision, no one else's. You might have experienced tremendous loss, hurt, and sickness, but you can still choose to live a life with joy in it—even through the sad and hard times.

Maybe that sounds cliché. Maybe you've heard "joy is a choice" a million times. But I want you to really hear me on this, so I'll say it again: It's *your* choice. It's up to *you*, and no one else. No one else is responsible for making you happy or fulfilled. Not your husband, not your mama, not your kids, not your best friend, not even the girl behind the counter at Baskin-Robbins (although, admittedly, she does a very good job serving up short-term joy experiences).

Joy is a one-woman job. We have to quit blaming our circumstances and the people around us for why we do not have joy. It is a *decision* to continually exist in sadness, and it is a decision to step out of that sadness.

Did that feel like I just ripped a strip of wax off your upper lip? I'm so sorry.

But honestly, I want to stand on the top of roofs and yell it out: *You can choose to be happy!* Because, my sweet, precious friend, you *can*.

Have you ever been around a miserable, mean person? Someone who emits real negativity, and when you're in their space it kind of sucks the life out of you? It's as if they're a black hole that might drag you in if you get too close, so something in you says to stay away. (I'm not saying you *should* stay away; this person probably needs you to take her to lunch or at least to give her this book.) That is a person who chooses over and over to stay in their pain. It may have been one big choice or a million little ones, but each time the chance to choose joy arises, the decision is made, instead, to continue down the path of hurt and bitterness.

Now, let's be clear: I am *not* saying we aren't meant to experience sadness or grief. Of course we are. I am also not speaking to those who suffer with debilitating mental illness or chronic depression. But for many people, there comes a point in your journey of pain and loss when you have to make a choice between embracing happiness or staying in your despair. If you want to climb out of the darkness—out of that pit of sadness—you have to be purposeful about it.

IF YOU WANT TO CLIMB OUT OF THE DARKNESS, YOU HAVE TO BE PURPOSEFUL ABOUT IT.

Many years ago I went to my first radiation appointment. I was nine months into my breast cancer treatments, and radiation was the final phase. Six weeks earlier I'd had my mastectomy, and for six awful months before that I'd endured chemotherapy. The first signs of hair were beginning to grow on my head, and I was oh-so-ready for this final stretch.

I arrived at the treatment center and was sent into a dressing room. I took off my shirt and bra and put on one of those incredibly attractive hospital gowns that ties in the back but never seems to work correctly, so you constantly fear a bit of naked is showing through. Praying that nothing too upsetting was hanging out, I entered the pretreatment waiting area and sat down.

Directly across from me was a woman who appeared to be in her late fifties. She had all her hair, had a plump figure, and her face was full of healthy color. She looked at me and asked, "Is this your first radiation treatment?"

I nervously nodded.

"Well, I have to tell you, it's hard," she said. She let out a big sigh. "The first week you will feel fine, and then you're going to get incredibly tired and you won't be able to function, and your skin is going to be so burned you won't be able to wear clothes. I don't even know how much more of this I can take."

I was stunned. That wasn't at all what I was expecting. My

oncologist had assured me that this was the easy part. Had he lied just to keep me going?

The woman told me she was seventeen rounds in and had only three more to go. I needed thirty-three, and her uplifting chat was sending me into full radiation freak-out mode.

About two minutes later, they called me back. I entered the room and lay down on the table. The technician marked up my breast with a Sharpie and aimed the radiation machine at my chest. The machine was on for eleven seconds in three different angles and I was done. Two minutes, tops. That was it.

The next day I returned, same routine, only this time sitting across from me was a frail, bald, white woman who looked painfully thin. I couldn't tell her age because she was in the throes of such sickness, but I would have guessed around seventy. She smiled immediately, her sickly face brightening as she said hello.

"How many rounds have you done?" she asked.

"One," I replied cautiously, fearful to hear another horror story of what was ahead.

She waved her hand like she was shooing a fly. "Oh, honey, this is nothing. It's a breeze. Today is my last round of thirty-three. Compared to what we've been through, this is a walk in the park."

I wanted to let out a burst of relief tears but managed to hold it together. As we talked a little more, I learned she had been battling cancer for years, in and out of hospitals, and yet I could see the way she chose to be a joyful light to others.

One chose joy, one chose misery. Physically, this second woman was suffering more than the previous day's lady, but nonetheless she chose to find the light in her day. She chose to lift me, even in the midst of her pain.

ONE CHOSE JOY. ONE CHOSE MISERY.

It would take almost an entire year before I fully understood the significance of her choice to speak with joy. That is when I too reached thirty-three rounds of radiation. I found myself exactly where that kind, frail woman must have been that day; I was exhausted, tired of being tired, and my skin was burned and blistered so badly that even the slightest brush of fabric was excruciating. I realized she must have been feeling just like this, and yet she had spoken to me with a smile, breathing belief into me, even through her own suffering.

Finding joy in your life does not mean you walk around in a perpetual state of skipping and laughing. It doesn't mean you are grinning and waving to every single passerby, although that would be fun. It means when you are sitting in the pain, you can take a deep breath and smile because God gave you one more breath to *live*.

> **WHEN YOU ARE SITTING IN THE PAIN, YOU CAN TAKE A DEEP BREATH AND SMILE BECAUSE GOD GAVE YOU ONE MORE BREATH TO *LIVE*.**

When my daughter Madison died, I didn't think I would ever be able to survive the intense, excruciating pain that came hand in hand with her death. It wrecked me down to my core, and it took me months before I thought I would even breathe normally again. The pain felt like a black cloak hanging on me, one I couldn't take off no matter how hard I tried. And I'll be honest, for a while I quit trying. Instead, I sat back and decided the black cloak was there to stay, and I just had to wear it.

As I began to look at what I was left with, I searched for just one thing I could feel grateful for. I had another daughter, so it seems like that would have been an easy answer. But when you are hurting so intensely, the obvious isn't so obvious and what might be possible feels impossible. Happiness seemed impossible.

But there she was, a bouncing, energetic, joyful three-year-old. My Makenzie. I knew she deserved more. She deserved a joyful mother. I didn't realize it at first, but recognizing this was the first small step toward climbing out of my hellacious pain—the first hint that I would eventually remove the black cloak.

At first my smiles were forced, my expressions of happiness were fake—all disguises of my horrific pain. Then one day, they weren't. They were how I authentically felt. I didn't notice it immediately when it happened; I just looked back one day and saw that in all the pain, happiness had found its way through.

I chose to model for Makenzie a parent who was happy and joy-filled, rather than one who was continually gripped in sadness, hiding in the sheets of her bed. I chose to get up, to laugh with her, to take and pick her up from school. It wasn't easy, but I was determined. I saw a counselor and I took medicine. I did everything I could to try to be what she deserved.

I would love to tell you that my reason was because I knew God created me for more or because I knew I needed to live my best life, but it wasn't. My reason for taking those first few steps to move out of sadness was just one—deciding to rediscover joy for the sake of my little girl—and it was enough.

My faith was not strong in this season. In fact, I had moved further away from God than ever. I was angry that God had not saved my innocent, beautiful Madison, that other children were miraculously healed and mine was not. Why did miracles happen every day but not for my baby? What kind of God would do this? I did not think He was a God of good; He let my baby die. My daughter was gone, and with her loss, my faith was gone too.

It took me many years to find my way back to Him, and now I know this is partially why it took me so long to find any joy after losing Madison. (But I also know that, even then, He was under that dark cloak with me. I just couldn't see Him.)

I do not have a perfect plan for finding joy, but for me, it has always started small. What am I grateful for? I know, seriously overused move, isn't it? But it works. I believe gratitude is the greatest catalyst for living a happy life.

There have been seasons when I've lain in bed and thanked God for my breath as tears streamed down my face. Literally, my breath. That I was alive, that He pulled me through another day of chemo.

Even now, there are days when I am frustrated and sad beyond comprehension that my sister is gone and I will have to grow old without her. The heartache may never disappear; the loss of those we cherish will always be part of who we are. But I choose to couple that sadness with joy—to lift up her memory in celebration, in gratitude for the years we had and the gift she was to me. I choose to let her beautiful face be a reminder of how our time here is fleeting and we cannot be complacent in our lives and our relationships.

JOY STARTS SMALL.

You might be reading this book because you're struggling to find joy. For some, you're feeling stuck in a rut that's formed from stress or boredom or busyness or inertia. For many of you, though, you're in the middle of physical or emotional pain, and you can't imagine feeling moments of happiness again. I am here to tell you this: What you have been through won't pass, but your feelings can pass. And when you're ready, they will change. Healing is possible.

HEALING IS POSSIBLE.

I know it sounds strange, but I wish everyone could experience devastating heartache. It's not that I want anyone to hurt, but I know it has been in my pain that I have found an abundance of laughter and joy. I found a faith and a relationship with God that guides my life today.

I promise you, joy and God are one and the same. My joy increased as my faith did; they went hand in hand. It might sound hokey and a little crazy, but I am living proof. When I chose to walk with God, when I gave my life over to Him and accepted Jesus Christ as my Lord and Savior, joy was easier. When you choose Him, you choose joy.

My faith has grown bit by bit. I don't understand the Bible fully, and I am not an angelic woman ready to eloquently share the perfect words of Scripture for every situation. But I've spent a ridiculous amount of time in the field getting on-the-job training about God and joy, and I know that I know that I know:

Joy, my sweet friend, is *your* choice. It can be a little choice or a big choice, but it is yours and yours alone.

EPILOGUE

It's a Real-Life Miracle

Now to him who is able to do immeasurably
more than all we ask or imagine, according
to his power that is at work within us.

EPHESIANS 3:20

YES, I WROTE A book because God told me to. Stop it. I
can see you rolling your eyes. I am well aware that telling the world
that God told me to write a book is . . . well, it'll get you a first-class
ticket on the crazy train.

But don't worry, because when God speaks, you're blanketed
in an undeniable, unambiguous covering of peace. You know every
single step to take and exactly what the journey will look like. A God

calling surpasses all understanding, all questioning, and all fear to move forward—because *God told you to do it.*

Yeahhh, not so much. (It'd be nice, though, right?) Let me tell you how my God calling *really* happened.

First, I think it's important to establish that God does not speak to me through burning bushes or angels on high. I'm a seriously flawed, messy woman, and I'm still growing into my faith more and more as each day passes. I am passionate about God, Jesus, and the Holy Spirit. (If I am freaking you out now, it's okay. Keep reading and I'll freak you out a little more.) For me, God is a constant in my life. He is in my thoughts, and He is in the whispers. He's the subtle voice in my mind, guiding me through my days.

But God is God, and sometimes when the whispers aren't working, He is loud and downright bossy. That is precisely how He told me to write a book, just after midnight one November evening.

For the week preceding this night, my body had been in an insane routine of waking at 12:30 A.M., tossing, turning, sweating, freezing, overthinking, worrying, and then finally going back to sleep three hours later. The pattern was exhausting. On this night, it started again.

I was 478 degrees, and my mind was racing. But this time I was *not* getting up. I was going to lie there, and I was going to fall back asleep no matter what. This premenopausal traitor of a body of mine would not win. We were sleeping.

And yet my mind wouldn't stop. *I bet I could refinish the kitchen cabinets myself. I don't need to hire anyone; I can do that. How hard can it be? I'll need power tools. Oh, and a paint gun! Yes! Tools! I wonder if they're on sale. I bet they'll be on sale for Black Friday. I love the sales. I hate the lines. I hate the crowds. I like to be alone. I recharge alone. Does that make me an introvert?*

Seven thousand crazy thoughts and ideas in 180 seconds. Typical night.

Then it all stopped, and a voice in my head said, *Dawn, you are going to write a book.* There was a pause, and then, in case I'd missed it the first time . . .

GOD: "Dawn, you are going to write a book."
I started to argue, because, you know, it makes total sense to
    argue with God when He is telling you to do something.
DAWN: "I can't write a book; I don't even read books. I like
    audiobooks." (Seriously, does He even know me?)
GOD: . . .
DAWN: "I really can't write a book. I'm busy. I'm redecorat-
    ing." (For the record, redecorating a house is seriously
    time-consuming.)

GOD: "Here are the chapters."

The ideas began flying through my mind. I could see story
     after story coming together.

GOD: "Write them down."

DAWN: "No, I'm tired."

GOD: "Write them down."

DAWN: "*Fine!* I will write them down. But I'm *really* tired."

I sat up, grabbed my phone, opened the Notes app, and
     started to write them down. I hit "Done" and lay back
     down.

DAWN: "Now can I go to sleep?"

GOD: "No, I have another chapter. Write it down."

DAWN: "But, God, I'm tired. Can I *please* go to sleep?"

GOD: "Write it down."

Admittedly, this interaction was mostly weird, but the next part
was just beautiful. I couldn't hear His voice anymore, but I could *see*
moments of my life.

The sweet face of my daughter Madison, who died when she
was nine months old. The verdict pronounced at the jury trial of
my rapist. My ex-husband giving me a conciliatory smile before we
were divorced. Moments of unexpected encouragement during
my cancer journey. Squeezing my mom's hand in the ICU after

her brain aneurysm. Sharing belly laughs with my sister, Kim, whom I had lost ten months earlier to cancer. All of it softly swirling in my mind.

I knew what it all meant; it was crystal clear. God wanted me to tell my stories and show how I had found joy and laughter through an often-heartbreaking life journey. I was supposed to share it with humor and just be myself.

Deciding to walk away from a lucrative career to write was a massive—almost ridiculous—leap of faith. The days and weeks and months following that night have been filled with questions, frustrations, and doubts. But they've also unfolded with immeasurable amounts of joy. I've learned I *have* to keep stepping forward, even when I'm not sure where I'm headed. I'm learning day by day that God is working in my life, even when I can't see it, and those sprinkles of joy along the way are His gifts, mine for the taking. I just have to choose to grab hold of them.

I've come to see the writing of this book you hold as a real-life miracle—and not just because I got woken up in the middle of the night with its table of contents. It's the fact that God is using those times when I thought my ugly cries couldn't get any uglier—and how remembering them all and writing them down as a gift for *you* has actually been a gift for *me*.

But here's the thing—I know God can do the same transforming miracle in your life that He did in mine. Maybe thoughts are swirling through your head right now, reminding you of the times He's been with you in the dark. Or maybe you're feeling hope that things can change—that what seems like a lifetime of grief could spark joy for the first time. This, my friend, is a real-life miracle, like a spring in the desert or water changing to wine. Take hold of it. Draw life from it. Don't let go. God is bringing water to your desert, even now.

You turned my wailing into dancing;

you removed my sackcloth and clothed me with joy,

that my heart may sing your praises and not be silent.

LORD my God, I will praise you forever.

PSALM 30:11–12

MY HEARTFELT THANKS

CRAIG—MY LOBSTER, MY LOVE, my darling husband. When I told him I needed to write the acknowledgments for this book, he said, "What's to write? Just say I owe it all to my husband and ghostwriter, Craig." That statement is particularly humorous because he hasn't read this book, much less written it. He has read his chapter, but nothing else, and as usual, he made me laugh out loud with such a statement; this is so much of why I love him.

Honey, thank you. Thank you for all of it, especially for standing by me, and often carrying me while I took a giant leap of faith to write this book. You are my perfect partner, and I can't imagine a single day of this journey without you. Thank you for living out life in such a beautiful way that you continually make my dreams come true. I love you.

Makenzie and Ellason—My precious daughters, you are my reason. It's that simple. My love for the two of you is the driving force that pushed me to write this book and anything else I've ever done. I don't know what I ever did so right in this life to get to be your mom, but I'm eternally grateful for it. No matter what you ever face in your lives, know that you are my joy, and I love you with every fiber of my being. I'll love you forever. I'll like you for always.

Mom—you are joy personified and one of my greatest life-gifts. Thank you for thinking that everything I do is fantastic and brilliant, even when it isn't. You are the best mom and friend, and I thank God for saving you every day because there's no one in the world I'd rather ride a fast Gator with than you!

Dad—I didn't know a daughter could fall more in love with her father with each passing year, but I do. Thank you for moving next door, having coffee with me almost daily, and helping me hide packages from Craig. You are the most wonderful dad in the world, and I love you so much.

Rosalie, mom—Thank you for raising this incredible man and loving me as your daughter.

Jodie—my best friend and sister; we've laughed and cried these last eighteen months, but mostly laughed at our own jokes because, let's be honest, we are the funniest people we know. Thank you for your unconditional belief and tireless pep talks. Together we will change the world . . . prolly.

Chloe, Kyla, Sawyer, and Sutton—Gigi wanted to make *sure* your names are in the book! I love you all to the moon and back; you always make me laugh and remind me what life is all about! Landon, you know I love you, too, sweet son-in-love.

Brenella and Mike Domingue (a.k.a. Nanny and Uncle Mike)— Your love and belief in me could quite literally move mountains. I will work for the rest of my life to prove you right. I love you so much and wish you'd move next door too.

The rest of the Clampetts, my family—Uncle Darryl, Kathy, Scott, Katie, Carter, and Nanny Sue, you always make me laugh and bring the best foods. Never stop!

Shari Shallard—Let's be honest; without you, there would be no book. Well, there may be a book, but it would have been terrible. Together we wrote a book, and this will always be ours. God brought you to me because he knew I did not know big words and that my writing needed a lot of work. Thank you for teaching me, editing me, and guiding me; I love you, Shari-the-Editor.

To the women in my life who would probably "help me hide a dead body," if need be—my dearest girlfriends Kali Brigham, Wendy Presley, Casie Hembree, Bridget Shaw, Stephanie Coker, Charlotte Donoso, Caroline Boudreaux, Kelli Cooper Pipkin, and

Kimi Steinberg, thank you for being the most fantastical women I've ever met. You are magnificent.

Paula Kasabian—You've been by my side through so much. Thank you for your unwavering love, your coffee deliveries, taking my newborn when I needed sleep, and for a beautiful friendship. I love you, too, Michael.

Karen Ridle—Thank you for always speaking to my soul and for being there for me through this. Your prayers, your guidance, and your love have meant so much to me.

Kathy Helou—Those weekly director calls that I thought were so annoying because of all that "Scripture stuff" opened the door to show me how to have a relationship with Jesus and changed my life eternally; I love you with all my heart.

The phenomenal women of the Power Unit, hands down the greatest group of women ever to come together—I am forever grateful for you, and I really miss you!

To my Mary Kay Pink Sisters and the Helou Area—My life was abundantly blessed by you, and I will forever be grateful for your love and friendship.

My Life Group—You listened to *a lot* of weekly ups and downs for a long time. Thank you for your limitless God belief and encouragement. I love you, Tracy Purdy, Melissa Shoemaker, Kristeen

ACKNOWLEDGMENTS

Kidd, Julia Dancaescu, Ali Hill, and Jenny Kunz, for putting up with me the longest.

My Pastors Joe and Suzannah Driver, and Echo Life Church—I will always cherish your many prayers and friendship.

Ashley Cochrane—No question that God brought us together for such a time as this. Thank you for the incredible photos in this book and your passion for sharing this story. I love you.

Emily Ley—My sweet friend, thank you for going before me and guiding me through the process of sharing my first book with the world. So grateful for countless conversations, nudging me to the Gift Division, and especially your belief and love in me. Having you there during my first book was a beautiful gift from God.

Lara Casey Isaacson—We go back a long way, and oh how we have changed. I never imagined you would be such a big piece of my story so many years later, but I'm so glad God knew. Thank you for guiding me, listening to me, and connecting me with Claudia. I love you, and I can't wait to see what the next thirteen years bring us.

Lauren Fennell-Cutter—It's all fun and games to thank everyone, but let's be honest, none of this would have happened if I had had bad hair. Thank you for fantastic hair and for being my sweet friend for so many years.

To my glorious saint of a literary agent, Claudia Cross—You are the best of the best. Thank you for putting up with countless ugly cries from me as I ventured into the unknown world of publishing. I adore you and thank you for taking my hand and leading me through this step-by-step. I couldn't have done it without you.

Adria—Probably the most excellent acquisitions editor the world has ever seen, but I may be a little biased. Thank you for saying yes to the book, thank you for believing in me, thank you for fighting for it, and thank you for being my friend.

My team at Thomas Nelson—In the history of publishing, never before has there been such a glorious collection of creative, brilliant, hardworking, funny, and godly people to put out one little ol' book. Thank you for putting so much love and effort into this book and believing so much in me.

My dearest Kim—I will tell your story all the days of my life; until we see each other again in heaven, I love you. Your big sister.

FINISHED THE BOOK AND LOOKING FOR A WAY TO LAUGH THROUGH THE UGLY CRY?

Catholic Lite

With your own pain and seasons of tears, how did joy and laughter sneak in through the cracks for you? How did it surprise you and give you the gift of relief you didn't think you'd ever have again?

I'm Not Your Girl

Has there been a time when you felt God was calling you to something you felt unqualified to do or be, either in a whisper or in a bold, loud push? What was it? Did you follow the calling?

If not, why? Do you feel God is calling you now to do something extraordinary?

Cancer Schmancer

Oftentimes, we create our own narrative. Is there a story in your head that plays over and over? What are ways you can change the story in your head? What habits can you start today that will change this story?

A Nice Round Head

What scars have you been hiding? Do you believe that sharing what holds you back can be a blessing to others? When others have shared their scars with you, how has it blessed your life? Does it make you feel braver to share your own?

The Joy in Getting Lucky

Sometimes we overlook the little things that bring joy. Gratitude doesn't need to be grand in size. Little wins make up the great big wins. Take some time to write down some of the small victories you've had and share them. Strive to make this a weekly practice.

You Get To

What daily tasks or responsibilities in your life feel like burdens or annoyances? What if you no longer had the ability to perform those tasks or those responsibilities were gone? Would it change your perspective on how you look at them? Sometimes we need a reminder that we must do the work in order to enjoy the things we love.

She's Still Your Friend

Think about your closest friends. Don't focus on their shortcomings or how they may have let you down in the past. Think about how they are truly gifted. Looking at someone from a different perspective allows us to give more grace during those times when we all fall short. What gifts and friends have you overlooked?

The Joy in Exercising

What physical activity makes you feel joyful? Not something you read or watch, but **do**. How can you make exercising more enjoyable?

Maybe She's Bad at Math?

We all have God-given gifts that we should be proud of. What are some of yours? If you get stumped on this one, ask your family and friends.

Mom's Red-Hot Toenails

When you think about the times you laughed the most, what are they? Are there commonalities among them? Perhaps people, places, or situations? Get out the Kleenex, share your favorite moments, and be prepared to laugh through the ugly cry.

My Lobster

Are there life-changing events in your life that are beyond your control? Sometimes we don't even realize we're **still** trying to control these events. Share what's going on, and ask for help to surrender control of it. When we share our fears and pains, it makes the load so much lighter and others can help us breathe and let go of what is out of our control.

Kim's RAK

Each of us holds the key to changing the world; we each can do small, random acts of kindness for others. What is a small act of kindness you can do for someone today? Imagine how it would feel to bless others several times this week! Then keep it going. Has someone blessed you with a RAK recently?

#KIMSMILLION

Are there tragedies in your life that brought you joy, not at the moment, but sprinkled throughout that season? Can you look back and see how God spread His love around the pain of it? Were there specific people God placed in your life during that season? What lessons did you learn?

It's a One-Woman Job

When you reflect on your life, how do you view where you are today on your faith journey? Can you see the winding road, the ups and downs, and how God is creating the beautiful tapestry of your life?

ABOUT THE AUTHOR

DAWN BARTON IS A former Olympic Curling champion and the face of many *Sports Illustrated Swimsuit Issues*. After successful careers in curling and modeling, Dawn found a passion for the Didgeridoo. When she is not in Alaska training to compete in the Iditarod with her dogs, Skye and Livvy, Dawn teaches the Didgeridoo to children around the world. She is also a highly accomplished culinary master and a recipient of the Fields Medal, a prestigious award in the field of mathematics.

Most of all, Dawn enjoys a good laugh. None of the above accolades are real, other than the names of her dogs. In real life Dawn is an author, speaker, wife, mom, and grandmother. Her extraordinary journey has also made her a self-proclaimed Joyologist. She lives with her husband, Craig; her daughter; her parents; Craig's mom; two horses; four dogs; and two cats in Florida. You can find her on any given day in a perpetual ponytail and a yoga outfit that has never been to yoga.

Before taking a giant leap of faith to write this book, Dawn enjoyed a thirty-year career in sales and marketing; and the last ten of those years were in direct sales. Dawn was a top-ten sales director for one of the world's biggest direct sales brands. In 2018 she left that career to follow a calling from God to share her stories and joy with the world.

Having achieved happiness and success in even her darkest days, Dawn believes in the power of finding joy through difficulty; each obstacle should not be a cause to quit but rather another reason to be triumphant.

For a little more joy, connect with Dawn on Instagram and Facebook @dawnrbarton or her website, dawnbarton.com.